THE GREATEST BEER RUN EVER

A Crazy Adventure In A Crazy War

John "Chick" Donohue
and JT Molloy

monoray

First published in Great Britain in 2020 by Monoray,
an imprint of Octopus Publishing Group Ltd
Carmelite House
50 Victoria Embankment
London EC4Y 0DZ
www.octopusbooks.co.uk

An Hachette UK Company
www.hachette.co.uk

First published in paperback in 2021

First published in the US in 2020 by arrangement with
William Morrow, an imprint of HarperCollins Publishers,
New York, New York U.S.A

ISBN 978-1-91318-331-8

A CIP catalogue record for this book is available from the
British Library.

Printed and bound in the UK

10 9 8 7 6 5 4 3 2 1

Map design: Adam Cross (adamcrossartwork.com)
Photo consultant: Gretchen Viehmann (hissingvulture.com)

This FSC® label means that materials used for the product have
been responsibly sourced

MIX
Paper from
responsible sources
FSC
www.fsc.org
FSC® C104740

FOR THERESA O'NEILL DONOHUE
AND FOR GEORGE RUSH AND EAMON RUSH

CONTENTS

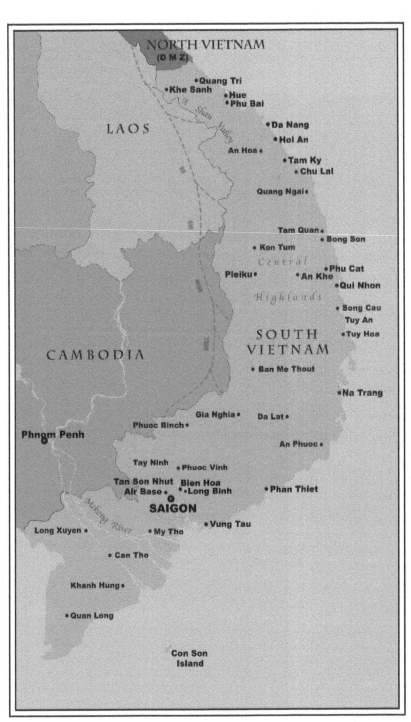

INTRODUCTION

In November 1967, John "Chick" Donohue was a twenty-six-year-old US Marine Corps veteran working as a merchant seaman, when he was challenged one night in a New York City bar. Chick and his friends were there, as ever, for the *craic*, where the stories and jokes told usually ended in a tide of laughter. Theirs was a pub tradition brought by their ancestors from Ireland, Scotland, Wales, and England here to Inwood, the idyllic northernmost neighborhood of Manhattan, where streets connected two rivers to the virgin forest that was once home to the Lenape Indians.

But the mood that night was somber. The men gathered in the bar had lost family and friends in the ongoing war in Vietnam.

Now, in an increasingly divided country, these men were seeing anti-war protesters—including some of their own brothers and sisters—turn on the troops as they showed up at the draft board when called. These boys, volunteering for the military or doing what they felt was their duty after being drafted into the US Army, were eighteen, nineteen years of age. They were met by signs emblazoned with slogans such as "GIs ARE BABY KILLERS" alongside other signs blasting US President Lyndon Johnson and his top general, William Westmoreland. At this point, Chick felt the protesters were traitors.

One of the guys in the bar that night proposed an idea many might deem preposterous: one of them should sneak into Vietnam, track down their buddies in combat, and give each of them a beer, a bear hug, laughs, and words of support from back home. Chick volunteered for the mission.

Thus began his odyssey, which would stretch from Qui Nhon Harbor and up north to the tense demilitarized zone, or DMZ, pushing against North Vietnam and Laos; to the Central Highlands along the border of Cambodia; to the US military's huge bull's-eye of an ammunition depot at Long Binh; and then all the way south to Saigon, the capital of South Vietnam—all in search of his friends.

Things did not go exactly as planned. Chick got caught up in the Tet offensive, in which North Vietnamese army soldiers and Viet Cong (VC) guerrillas invaded a hundred towns and key military sites, including the capital. Blowing up the ammo depot and other installations, they battled for two months. His buddies were thrown into the fighting, and Chick himself was by chance in one of the most strategic locations as Tet began. In hiding right outside the US embassy, Chick witnessed the embassy's seizure by just nineteen VC guerrillas, and the fight to take it back by a few young military policemen, marines, and chopper pilots. The seizure shocked Americans, and caused top newsman Walter Cronkite to fly to Vietnam and declare that the war could not be won. President Johnson concluded, "If I've lost Cronkite, I've lost Middle America," and announced his abandonment of a reelection bid.

After Chick stood outside the US embassy as a few boys fought and died to take it back, and heard General Westmoreland's later statements to the press about "the enemy's well-laid plans" going "afoul", he started to question the official line. The official reports didn't jibe with what he had witnessed. Chick emerged from his odyssey a changed man.

"Gradually," Chick says in the Afterword to this book, "I began to see that the protesters, however disrespectfully, were at least trying to stop this madness... If there is one thing I that learned as a result of my Vietnam experience it's that government—all governments for that matter—are not to be trusted. Many politicians lie when it serves their interests."

Chick Donohue is a true one-off. Later in life he became a tunnel worker. As a rep for his union in Washington, he once brought several US Senators seven hundred feet below the sidewalks in a cage elevator into the dripping caves. He didn't bring them back up again until they pledged to vote to fund jobs on infrastructure projects. During the bitter 1990 *New York Daily News* strike, when he was working for the Teamsters, who supported the strikers, Chick found out that a freight train full of newsprint paper from Canada was headed to New York so that management could publish a "scab paper." Chick paid a visit to workers at an upstate train yard, and, somehow, the train was intercepted and "got lost". In North Dakota.

And when his friend the author Frank McCourt, whose bestselling memoir *Angela's Ashes* recounted his impoverished upbringing primarily in Ireland, received threats before he was to give a public reading in Ireland, Chick flew over with a hulking alleged New York mobster to stand next to McCourt as he read. There was no trouble.

You get the picture. Chick is the subject of many an amazing story, but the one you are about to read is the best.

—JTM

THE
GREATEST
BEER RUN
EVER

The Hedgehog Inn in Inwood, one of the bars regularly frequented by Chickie. It has been estimated that at the time there were as many as a hundred bars in an approximately twelve-square-block radius in the Inwood neighborhood.

CHAPTER 1

ONE NIGHT IN A NEW YORK CITY BAR—THE COLONEL'S CHALLENGE

We were in Doc Fiddler's one cold night in November 1967. It was a favorite bar in the Inwood neighborhood of Manhattan, at 275 Sherman Avenue, above Isham Street. George Lynch was the bartender. We called him the Colonel. It was an honorary title, since he had made only private first class in the army. But he was a great military historian and patriot.

One day the Colonel commandeered the empty lot on the corner and erected a gigantic flagpole—something you might find in Central Park or in front of a government building. It's still there. Every morning, he would ceremoniously raise the flag; every sunset, he would lower it. Each Memorial Day and Fourth of July, the Colonel would organize a parade up Sherman Avenue. He tapped his connections to make it huge. He got Bill Lenahan, who was the commanding officer of the US Marine Corps Reserve at Fort Schuyler, the nineteenth-century fort in Throggs Neck that's now home to the State University of New York's Maritime College and Museum, to literally send in the marines to march. The Colonel's efforts took on an even greater urgency now that we were at war in Vietnam and with so many of our neighborhood boys serving there.

The Colonel got Finbar Devine, a towering man who lived up the street and who headed the New York City Police Department (NYPD) Pipes and Drums of the Emerald Society, to lead the flying wedge of kilted bagpipers and drummers while wearing his plumed fur Hussar's hat and thrusting his mace heavenward. Father Kevin Devine, Finbar's brother and the Good Shepherd Parish priest, got all the priests and the nuns and the kids from the Catholic school to march, too. Another Devine brother was with the Federal Bureau of Investigation, and the Colonel convinced him to organize a contingent of FBI agents to come out from under cover and march. The Colonel was beautifully crazy.

He treated the boys who came back from the war like kings. At Doc Fiddler's, they didn't pay for a drink. Around the corner from the bar, in what we called the Barracks, he lived in a room with two army surplus bunk beds—one for himself and one for any GI who'd come home and needed a place to stay.

Behind the bar, the Colonel ruled. He listened and laughed and could tell a story like your Irish grandfather, doing every accent and voice, no word astray, with a finish that would cure your asthma laughing. But he was tough, and those who engaged in tomfoolery on his watch were soon jettisoned.

The Colonel had become unhappy lately with what he was seeing on news reports about the war. Antiwar protesters were turning anti-soldier. Not just anti–President Lyndon

Baines Johnson, who escalated the conflict he'd inherited from President John F. Kennedy by increasing the troops from JFK's sixteen thousand to half a million. Nor were they strictly focused on General William Westmoreland, commander of US forces in Vietnam, who was asking for even more troops to be deployed. Protesters were now training their sights on teenagers who'd been drafted, and on veterans who'd come home from a hell they couldn't express. We were told that when the neighborhood boys had gone down to the draft board on Whitehall Street—many so inexperienced that their fathers or older brothers accompanied them—they'd been met by picketers carrying signs that read, "GIs Are Murderers."

As these news scenes played out on the TV above the bar, the Colonel didn't hide his disgust.

"You know how demoralized they must be while they're over there doing their duty?" he would growl. "We've got to do something for them!"

"Yeah!" shouted the assembled.

"We've got to show them we support them!"

"That's right!!" came the shouts, even louder.

"Somebody ought to go over to 'Nam, track down our boys from the neighborhood, and bring them each a beer!"

"Yeah!!—Wait. *What?*"

"You heard me! Bring them excellent beer, bring them messages from back home. Bring them . . . encouragement. Tell them we're with them every step of the way!"

The Colonel folded his arms on the bar and looked me dead serious in the eyes. "Chickie," he said, "I want to borrow your seaman's card."

It sounded more like an order than a request.

I was a US merchant mariner, a civilian seaman working on tankers and other commercial ships. I had joined after serving in the US Marine Corps for four years into the early 1960s.

I had a seaman's card—it's called a "Z" card—which is like a military ID. It has your picture and years of service on it. Mine noted that I could handle ammo, because I had military clearance. It's issued by the US Coast Guard and used in lieu of a passport.

"What do you want my seaman's card for?" I asked.

"I'm gonna get on one of those ships that goes to Vietnam," he answered, "and I'm gonna bring all the guys over there from the neighborhood a drink."

During the war, civilians couldn't fly from the States to Vietnam without military orders—not that anybody wanted to take spring break in beautiful downtown Da Nang.

But there was no way the Colonel could "borrow" my seaman's card to sail off to the war zone. He wouldn't know what to do on a merchant ship. Besides, he didn't look anything like me. I had red hair, I was ten years younger—forget it, there was no way. Besides, the idea was insane. Wasn't it?

I looked in the Colonel's eyes to see if he could possibly be serious. Oh, he was.

As of late 1967, Inwood had already buried twenty-eight brothers, cousins, and friends who had been killed in Vietnam. People from the whole neighborhood would turn up for the funeral, whether they knew the boy or not. At least half of the soldiers had been drafted or signed up right after leaving high school at the age of eighteen or even seventeen. At seventeen, their parents had to sign a permission slip, like for a field trip in school—a nine-thousand-mile field trip from which they might never return. Of the young men who did go to college, many were drafted soon after graduation and could be drafted until the age of twenty-six.

In Inwood, you didn't have guys with a doctor friend of the family composing notes about nervous maladies or heel spurs. No guys playing the endless college-deferment game like future vice president Dick Cheney, with his four college deferments and another for good luck. For us, crossing the border and becoming Canadian wasn't an option, either.

The Colonel and I had been good friends with Mike Morrow. He had been killed in June at the age of twenty-two by a mortar in the battle of Xom Bo II. His company and three others from the First Infantry Division were ambushed and outnumbered at Landing Zone X-Ray by up to two thousand Vietcong (VC) soldiers. The bloody score, as reported by the United States government: "they" lost 222; we lost 39, just as the Summer of Love was getting started back home. We also lost Johnny Knopf at twenty-three, killed on All Saints' Day, November 1, 1966, when his mother was in church praying for him.

Then there was Tommy Minogue, who signed up at nineteen and one month; after turning twenty in March 1967, he had died a hero. His death was particularly hard to take. As courageous as Tommy was, he was a sweet kid. He was big, but he would never think of bullying anyone. He never wanted anybody to feel left out, and he found a way to include kids no one else would want to play with in the team sports in Inwood Park or in street games. We were friends with his older brother, Jack, and his three other brothers, so he was a little brother to us. Back then, when parents would have four or six or even ten kids, the older brothers would let the young ones tag along, and we'd look after all of them.

This was the kind of kid Tommy was: one summer, his father, John "One Punch" Minogue, asked his friend Danny Lynch down at the Miramar Pool if he had a job for Tommy, to keep him out of trouble for the ten long, hot weeks away from school. Lynch said he was sorry, but they'd filled all the jobs. Mr. Minogue looked dejected as he walked away.

Lynch called out, "Wait! Maybe Tommy could come and help out, and then he could at least swim for free."

Mr. Minogue went for it, and so did Tommy: He worked like a beaver every day. Lifeguard Andy Rosenzweig tells the story of how one day, the owner of Miramar Pool showed up as Tommy was sweeping and stacking towels and carrying deck chairs. He asked, "Wow, what are we paying that kid?" and Lynch replied, "Nothing."

"Well, start paying him today," the boss commanded. Even bosses saw Tommy's integrity.

Later, Tommy joined the Second Battalion of the Thirty-Fifth Army Infantry and became a platoon medic. He was soon sent to Kon Tum Province, in the Central Highlands, on Vietnam's border with Laos. A few days after Saint Patrick's Day, his unit of one hundred soldiers was surrounded by a thousand North Vietnamese army (NVA) regulars who had swarmed over the border. The platoon, outnumbered ten to one, was overrun within minutes, leaving company commander Captain Ronald Rykowski badly wounded. Tommy ran a hundred feet through a hail of bullets and threw his body over his captain, taking several bullets. Ignoring his own wounds, he treated the commanding officer, ultimately saving his life and that of the company radio operator next to him. Tommy then grabbed a machine gun from a fallen brother and fought back against the NVA soldiers, along with the remaining members of his company, continuing to shield the wounded Captain Rykowski. At the captain's orders, the radio operator called in air support, but by the time it came, twenty-two men had been killed and forty-seven badly wounded. Tommy didn't make it.

Three of his brothers, Jack, Donald, and Kevin, organized the Thomas F. Minogue Chapter of the Narrowbacks Social and Protective Club, and dozens of us meet regularly to remember him. I still don't know why Tommy Minogue hasn't been awarded the Medal of Honor, given by the president on behalf of Congress for extraordinary acts of valor.

These were the kinds of kids we were losing. They were so young—eighteen and nineteen, early twenties. The marines, which I'd joined at seventeen, considered me old at twenty-six; they'd cited my age as the reason for rejecting me when I'd tried to re-up in 1967.

People didn't support the troops then as much as they do now. The country seemed ungrateful for what they were doing, because it was an unpopular war, and Americans were watching its brutality on the television news every night. But our young soldiers were doing what they felt was their duty. I'm not saying every guy was gung-ho about going to fight the Vietnamese. But in our community, at that time, if you were called by your country to fight what our leaders said was the spread of Communism, you went. You wouldn't think of doing anything else but your duty. In Inwood, we grew up singing "The Star-Spangled Banner" at the end of Mass every Sunday; you'd receive Holy Communion and sing the "*Agnus Dei*" Latin hymn, and that would flow right into the national anthem like a medley. Your feelings of patriotism were connected to your religious beliefs. They were cut from the same sacred cloth.

The guys who didn't want to serve, they moved out of the neighborhood. If I truly believed how they believed, I would have left, too. I wouldn't want to make enemies of the people I grew up with because we disagreed about President Johnson, General Westmoreland, or Secretary of Defense Robert McNamara. The fight was with them, not the people on my block. You didn't have protests in Inwood.

I would see the protesters in Central Park, and if I became one of the guys yelling back at them, what would that accomplish? Nothing. But I wanted to do *something*. Having served in the marines overseas myself, I figured that when our buddies over there heard about the discord from new recruits or in letters from back home, it would probably make them feel pretty damn bad.

To us, the people marching here with the red-and-yellow North Vietnamese flag while our guys were over there dying were traitors. No matter how we felt about the war, that was just wrong. What we didn't know yet was that our own brothers and sisters were among the protesters, and that Vietnam veterans would soon join them. But rather than go down and fight the antiwar demonstrators, the Colonel wanted to launch his own counteroffensive and go directly to Vietnam to supply positive reinforcement to our boys.

"We gotta support them!" he yelled again.

I felt the same way as he did, but actually going there seemed a little extreme. I couldn't give the Colonel my seaman's card.

Two months before I left for Vietnam I was feeling rather carefree: no shoes, no shirt, no helmet.

And I had been "on the beach"—slang for not working on a ship—for a while now. I was doing nothing, simply hanging out and drinking beer with my buddies, while our friends were over there dying or wounded or in harm's way.

I thought, *I have the right ID papers to slip into Vietnam as a civilian. I have the time. Maybe I can do this. No: I have to do this. Some authority figures will probably stop me, but I have to try. I have to.*

"Yeah, George, okay," I said. "You get me a list of the guys and what units they're with, and the next time I'm over there, I'll bring them all a beer."

It was sort of a flippant thing to say, but that's how it all started.

CHAPTER 2

GATHERING THE NAMES

The next day, I went into the bar and found that word had gotten out. People young and old came with slips of paper and letters with names of units or military postal addresses they had for their sons or brothers or cousins serving over there. When you wrote letters to soldiers in Vietnam, you would write their unit care of San Francisco, and the army, navy, air force, or marines would find them. You didn't want to give the enemy crib notes should the mailbag tumble out of the chopper. But the patrons told me the strange names of the places their boys had been: Phuoc Long, Binh Dinh, Pleiku, Lam Dong. I was a bit overwhelmed and jotted it all down, stuffing the precious pages into my pockets.

Amidst all the noise, I saw Mrs. Collins, hovering inside the front door. She was with her son Billy, or should I say, Chuckles. (Once he started laughing, he couldn't stop, no matter what nun or cop was giving him the stink eye, hence the nickname. The only people who called him William or Billy were his parents and substitute teachers.) Chuckles had been one of my best friends since grade school, so I knew Mrs. Collins, and she was never one to set foot in a pub.

However, her younger son, Thomas Collins, was stationed in Vietnam. As soon as she spotted me, she approached me and said in her lilting brogue, "Billy tells me you're going over to see my Tommy! Oh, thank God for you, Chickie! Tell my Tommy how much I miss him! And tell him that I pray for him every single day!"

She gave me a hug and then tried to hand me $100 in small bills—to give to her son, or to buy him a drink, or to use myself for whatever I needed to make the trip, she said. But I knew that the second I took that money, I would be in for it. In the cold, sober light of day, I was having second thoughts. What the hell had I agreed to the night before? I declined, as much as I could have used that $100, because I didn't want to be obligated and then get killed trying to find Tommy Collins in Vietnam.

"Mrs. Collins," I said, "let me know Tommy's unit. I'll find him. And if I do, I'll tell him how much you love him."

The Colonel yelled, "Don't worry, Mrs. Collins! Chickie'll take care of it! He's gonna do this! Let's raise a glass to Chickie!"

"To Chickie!" the crowd cheered, though I could see some skeptical faces.

The Colonel poured me another beer, and I drank as I compiled a list, with Tommy Collins at the top. Some sidled up and told me what they knew of soldiers' whereabouts. Pally McFadden gave me his brother Joey's coordinates with the army. A brother of Rich Reynolds, a second lieutenant in the Marine Corps, gave me his last known location. Ed O'Halloran knew where Kevin McLoone was. Kevin and I used to rent

Winnebagos with a couple of other guys and go from Chambers Bar in Inwood to New York Giants football games—at home then in Yankee Stadium and sometimes hundreds of miles away. Kevin had already served in the marines in Vietnam; now he had gone back as a civilian to help outfit helicopters with new radio technology that would help prevent so many of them from getting shot down.

"Rick Duggan! You gotta find Rick!" someone shouted. "He's been all over the front lines!" Nobody knew what front line Rick was on at the moment, so I determined to go ask his parents. Rick had grown up in the same building as I had on the dead end of Seaman Avenue. His father was the only Republican in the neighborhood—and my aunt ran the Democratic club—but they joked about it. Rick and I were close; like Tommy, he was one of the younger, more fearless kids we let tag along with us when we dove off tall cliffs into the murky waters of the Spuyten Duyvil or generally caroused. Rick was with the First Air Cavalry Division and had joined at the age of nineteen. I planned to visit his parents the next day and ask for his location. I knew his grandmother had sent him a bottle of whiskey hidden—and cushioned—in a loaf of Wonder bread.

Of course, I would try to find my good buddy Bobby Pappas, with whom I had gotten into a shenanigan or two. His father tended bar down the block, so I'd ask him if he had any information. Bobby was in his midtwenties, married with a baby, and he had already served in the US Army Corps of Engineers, but he got drafted anyway, because LBJ had ended President Kennedy's mandate not to draft married fathers. I didn't think that was fair.

I took one last sip and headed out the door. The Colonel refused my money and shouted, "God bless Chickie, and God bless America!" and some guys yelled, "Yeah!" and "Go, Chick!" It was as if the Colonel had given me my orders, and off I was to go on my mission. There was only one problem:

I still had my doubts that I could pull it off.

CHAPTER 3

SETTING SAIL

The next day, I went down to the National Maritime Union Hall at Seventh Avenue and Thirteenth Street. This great union was started in 1936 by a brave boatswain—a deck boss—named Joseph "Big Joe" Curran. He was charged with mutiny by President Franklin Roosevelt's secretary of commerce after exhorting seamen on the SS *California* to refuse to cast off the lines until monthly wages were raised by $5. Seamen up and down the Eastern Seaboard went on strike, and Curran became president of the union. In addition to winning the forty-hour workweek and benefits, Big Joe built the hiring halls specifically to end corruption in filling jobs and to keep the workforce integrated. The NMU (now the Seafarers International Union of North America) has been very, very good to me and a lot of other mariners.

The union had built three modern buildings in the Chelsea neighborhood, on Manhattan's West Side, including the ship-like headquarters I was in, and a seamen's residence down the block with a hundred giant porthole windows, a pool, a gym, and classrooms. It's now the Maritime Hotel.

New York was still a thriving shipping port in the 1960s. At the hiring hall, they had a board listing which ships were in port and what positions were open: fireman, oiler, boatswain, deckhand, mechanic, and the like. If you were on the beach, and you were ready to go back out to sea, you would come down and sit in the auditorium with the other seamen, and the union port delegate would call out the names of the ships and their destinations. Like this: "The SS *Manhattan*!! Going to the Gulf!!!" That was one of Greek shipping tycoon Stavros Niarchos's oil tankers, headed back to the Persian Gulf for a fill-up. Or "The MS *Alameda*!!! Going coastwise!!!"—a merchant ship stopping at ports all along the US East Coast. They wouldn't give you a big description. In those days, the newspapers listed which ships were in port. If they called out Moore-McCormack Lines, or Mooremac, as we referred to it, chances were pretty good the ship was heading to South America from the Twenty-Third Street Pier in Brooklyn.

If you went to South America on a freight ship, you might leave that afternoon and be gone for four months. It's a big place, with a lot of ports. Before container shipping, it could take a week to unload the cargo and to refuel the ship's four or five oil tanks. That's why you would always know when a ship was leaving but not when it was arriving. In the States, the ship might pick up cargo in Brooklyn, stop in Philly to load up on more cargo, then head to Baltimore, Norfolk, Charleston, Savannah. Then it would go foreign, drop off and pick up cargo down the east coast of South America and return to the States. As soon as you were back in the good old USA, you would be paid. In cash.

I suddenly heard the word "victory" and snapped to attention. "The *Drake Victory!*" the guy yelled again, and I knew that it was probably headed to Vietnam. The great Victory ships of World War II were part of the "mothball fleet" that had been "Butterworthed"—cleaned spic-and-span—and pressed back into service in Vietnam, transporting everything from tanks to river barges. I jumped up.

Somebody yelled, "Pierhead!" That meant the ship was about to leave. I headed to the front of the hall. The ship was still short an oiler, but it was on a tight schedule and about to depart shorthanded. I was qualified to be an oiler—part of the "black gang" that worked below decks in the engine room—so I threw my card into the pile right then and there. I had seniority, and I'd been on the beach the longest, so I got the job. They told me to head directly to the ship from the hiring hall. Forget about long, tender good-byes.

I didn't have time to rush home. I had brought a duffel with me just in case, so I rushed up to Fourteenth Street and bought a razor, socks—just the essentials—threw them in the bag, and hustled uptown to the Port Authority Bus Terminal to catch the bus out to the ship. The SS *Drake Victory* was docked a few miles south of Staten Island, in Leonardo, New Jersey, where a milelong pier with three "fingers," or smaller piers, jutted into Raritan Bay.

When I arrived, it was hard to miss her, glinting in the sun, all 455 gorgeous feet of her. I was filled with pride looking at that ship. Americans built 531 Victory ships in six ship-yards in only twenty-one months during World War II. With their sharp-angled, raked bows and canoe sterns, plus powerful steam-turbine engines that gave them three times the horsepower of the Liberty ships that came before them, these speedier vessels were better able to evade the German U-boat

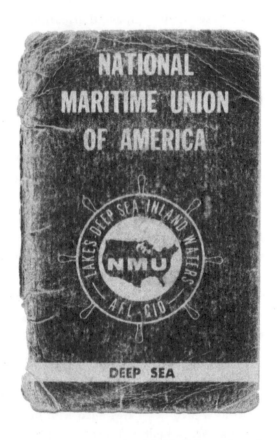

Deep Sea: My union book held all the credentials
I needed for seafaring.

submarines that torpedoed 138 of the Liberty ships—and 2,825 merchant ships overall—over the course of the war.

There was a bar near the dock. I ran in and asked the bartender to give me about a case of beer. When I told him where I was bringing it, he gave me a great price. I asked him to include New York brands such as Pabst Blue Ribbon, Schaefer, Schlitz, Piels, Ballantine, and Rheingold. I knew that since the Civil War, the US military has never been that far from beer. I'd already been to Vietnam twice as a seaman, and I felt assured that I could replenish my supply with the bigger American brands like Budweiser and Miller once I got there. But I wanted to bring some hometown favorites. I sure as hell wasn't about to go all that way to buy them the local Saigon swill. They have decent beer there now, but during the Vietnam War, one bottle might smell like vinegar, another like formaldehyde, another like the Harlem River. Then maybe you'd get a good one. That's why you had to drink three or four.

A dockworker saw me running and offered to give me a lift in his cart. I spotted a pay phone on the dock and said, "Thanks, Buddy, but do you mind if I make a quick call?" He said, "No problem," and waited.

I put in a dime and dialed my parents' number in New Jersey, where they had moved from Inwood to be closer to my father's two jobs. They had no idea I was taking off. It rang four times, and I was getting nervous that nobody was home, when I heard my mother's voice say hello.

"Ma, hi, it's me, Chickie."

"Chickie! Are you all right?"

"Yeah, Ma, I'm fine, but I'm headed out again. I just wanted to say so long to you."

"Chickie, where are you going?"

"Um, Asia, Ma, you know, like I was in the marines, and I'm going on a beautiful, old refurbished World War II Victory ship. Tell Dad; he'll like that. It's a cargo ship contracted to the navy."

"Can't you wait until after Thanksgiving, Chickie? I'm making the mushroom stuffing."

"My favorite! Put some of it in the freezer for me, Ma, and I'll have it when I come back. With a drumstick. Ships don't wait."

"Well, you be careful, Chickie. And don't do anything foolish. Try to send us postcards."

"Okay, Mom, you take care now. I'll be back before you can say, 'Go raibh an ghaoth go brách ag do chúl.'" She knew it meant "May the wind be always at your back" in our ancestral Irish, and that gave her a little laugh, which made me feel good.

I didn't dare mention Vietnam. I had made last-minute dockside calls to her before, but this was different: for the first time, I was scared. When I had been to Vietnam before as a mariner, I hadn't ventured much out of port and into the interior. This time I would, and I didn't know what I would find. The feeling lasted two or three minutes, but it was the only time I remember fearing that I might not come back to them. Yeah, I was scared, but I knew I had to try.

I hopped in the dockworker's cart, and off he sped. The *Drake* was about to sail, and when she did, I was on deck. One long blast sounded, and we set sail, headed out to sea for the journey south to the Panama Canal.

Well, I thought, *I'm on my way.* If I couldn't pull it off, at least I could say that I had tried.

CHAPTER 4

VOYAGE TO VIETNAM

Ammo ships are not like cruise ships. They don't stop in Miami or Cancún. They head way out into the ocean, beyond the territorial waters, sailing parallel to the coast but far from the busy harbors of cities. You never want to dock a ship full of bombs at a big port because if the ship should blow up at sea, at least the disaster wouldn't be compounded by casualties on surrounding boats or on shore. We left the States, sailed about twenty-five nautical miles out, and then due south.

The maximum speed of an ammo ship was about seventeen knots, on good seas; we usually cruised at about thirteen knots—on land that'd be about fifteen miles an hour. So, it took us five days to arrive at the port of Colón, Panama, on the Atlantic side of the canal. From there, the *Drake Victory* took on a canal pilot to sail her the forty-eight miles through the man-made waterway to Balboa, Panama, on the Pacific side. There we filled her with bunker fuel. She was barely "Panamax"—canal-size—and it was amazing to see her needle through locks 110 feet wide. It took more than a day, and the captain let us have shore leave.

Some of us took the parrot-colored Panama Canal Railway train, which runs parallel to the canal across the isthmus toward Balboa. Those hills are where privateer Sir Francis Drake ventured past the Spanish Main to climb a hilltop tree and become the first Englishman to see the Pacific Ocean. I figured the *Drake Victory* was named for him. He was soon plundering Spanish ships loaded with their own plunder: Incan silver and gold by the ton. Drake was the one who started the legal concept that a captain has absolute power on his ship: after he took a dislike to his co-commander, an aristocrat with strong ties to Queen Elizabeth I of England, he simply accused him of witchcraft and beheaded him. That's why I don't like ship captains: absolute power.

Even then, before I had ever worked as a sandhog, I was blown away by what the Panama Canal workers had achieved with nothing but shovels, their bare hands, dynamite, and a few turn-of-the-twentieth-century steam excavators. They had to cut through a spiny mountain in the Continental Divide and build a dam to divert a lake. I read that they excavated twenty-five times what other sandhogs dug out eighty years later for the Chunnel, the thirty-one-mile tunnel connecting England and France beneath the English Channel.

National Maritime Union regulations required that we be paid up to half our salary earned to the point when we went onshore. The US economy was so good then that American dollars went a long way in Panama. We had ourselves a good time in Balboa that night. I partied like it was my last trip, and I kind of felt like it might be. Still, I took comfort in the fact that I wasn't married then, nor did I have any kids. You're not as worried about dying when you're young and unattached.

We got back on board the *Drake Victory* for the monthlong voyage across the Pacific to Vietnam. We followed the equator most of the way, even though it took longer. With our cargo of ammo, we had to stay out of the shipping lanes. We didn't see a boat, we didn't see a plane, we never saw an island.

The ship had been taken out of mothballs and hadn't carried a crew since World War II. There were actually a few guys on the ship who had served in that war and had been asked to come out of retirement to show the young lads how to run these beauties. Some of them had lost buddies and survived on rafts and lifeboats after German submarines sunk their ships off the coasts of Europe, Asia, and even the States. U-boats had sunk 175 merchant ships sailing from ports in Virginia, Florida, Louisiana, North Carolina, and more on the West Coast. These ships brought essential cargo such as munitions, equipment, and supplies to Europe. In fact, World War II merchant mariners had a higher percentage of casualties—9,521 souls, according to merchant mariner historian Toni Horodysky—than any branch of the military. Yet they didn't receive any recognition or the benefits of the GI Bill, and they had to sue to receive Veterans Administration benefits more than forty years later, in 1988.

The ship was a 100 percent male world. There was no such thing as "Hey, watch your language." So, from the first union meeting, guys were marking out their territory. I had gotten myself elected the ship's union chairman. It was easy: nobody else wanted to fill out the forms. I had learned over the years that captains give union reps a wider berth. They didn't want grievances filed or anything that would tangle them up in the bureaucracy of hearings. I figured it would help me with time off the ship once we reached Vietnam, so I could do what I had to do.

As ship's chairman, I announced that the so-called black gang would take care of the engine room and environs, while the stewards would keep clean the officers' cabins and the rank-and-filers' fo'c'sles—short for forecastles, the sailors' sleeping quarters—and the main deck. Some guys had a whole fo'c'sle, with its four bunk beds, to themselves, because during World War II a Victory ship might have had seventy sailors on it, and we were a crew of only twenty-three.

The cook, who was in charge of the stewards, didn't like that division of labor. He was a big, tough guy, about six foot four, with a chef's toque perched on his huge Afro. "I'm not gonna let my workers clean up for a bunch of deck apes!" he yelled. We worked that one out, but tension continued between the departments during the sail about who was to chip, who was to paint, who was to do this or that.

Then one morning, we were about a thousand miles from land on a beautiful blue-sky day, so those of us not tending the engines were all out on deck. There wasn't a plane in the sky or another ship on the horizon. We were in the middle of the Pacific all by ourselves, when suddenly smoke started pouring out of one of the forward hatches. The hatch was a rectangular wooden opening as big as a car, covered with canvas to stop rain and seawater from pouring in below deck, but now it was burning.

"Fire!" somebody hollered. But we didn't know where it was. It could be the canvas covering the hatch, or it could be down in the hole. And we were standing on the deck of a ship loaded with ten thousand tons of ammunition. If the fire spread to the hold, we'd all be blown to kingdom come. The chef, the engineer, the boatswain, and the deck crew ran like hell toward the fire to put it out together. Nobody asked, "Whose job is this?" It was: *"Everybody put it out now!"* And we did. For the rest of the voyage, we all helped out one another.

I spent my days tending to the ship's 8,500-horsepower Lentz steam engine, oiling its huge wheel and all the other moving parts as the ship made its long, slow glide around the belt of the Earth. Time went by with the rhythm of the waves. The guys who join the merchant marines are a tough lot, because it can get lonely out there. Maybe that's why some of them sign up, like men who used to join the French Foreign Legion to forget someone. But mariners, in general, are men who love the sea. You have to love the sea almost more than you love a "normal" life on land with a family, because you're often gone for a long, long time.

There was not much to see, save for the rare whale off starboard or a flipper of something off port side. Otherwise, the only thing breaking up the dull buzz of the day would be a shout that signaled the end of a shift: four hours on, eight hours off, four hours on again, day after day for weeks. You always wanted to work overtime shifts if you could, because basic pay was only about $300 a month—about $2,218 before taxes today—and OT could boost it. I worked a lot of double shifts on the voyage, but not primarily for the cash; the seamen I'd traded hours with had agreed to cover for me when I went on my sojourn onshore. There was the occasional game of rummy or blackjack. Sometimes I'd go up on deck and peer at the unadorned horizon, mostly thinking of what lay ahead.

One day I was on deck, and those thoughts turned to Japan, probably because I'd sailed there on the troop ship the USS *Hugh Gaffey* after joining the marines. The military is like the lottery in determining where you serve, and, of course, your fate is also shaped by whether it's peacetime or wartime. Some guys spent their entire World War II service in Malibu, California. Others were stationed at a secret US Army Air Forces base in the Galápagos Islands, a beautiful, exotic place where the British naturalist Charles Darwin studied the rare giant sea tortoises and developed his theory of evolution. My brother, Billy, who had joined the marines the year before I did, spent three years in North Carolina. I served five months in the Philippine jungle and on Guantanamo in Cuba, before the Vietnam War.

I also got to serve in Japan. I won that crapshoot. I fell in love with a beautiful girl there named Michiko, which gave me an incentive to learn to speak Japanese and find out about Asian culture. That would come in very handy in Vietnam.

I was daydreaming about Michiko when I suddenly heard someone yell, "Land!" I snapped out of it as every free deck-hand on the *Drake Victory* scrambled up to take a look. There it was: no shapes of palm trees or huts to be seen, but it was land, all right—a dark-green mound way, way out where the sky met the sea.

"It's probably the Philippines," somebody said, sounding a little wistful. He must have been right, because a few days later, on January 19, 1968, after eight weeks at sea, we dropped anchor at South Vietnam's Qui Nhon Harbor.

Somewhere out there were the guys from my neighborhood, and it was time for me to find them.

Here I am in my days as a US Marine, stationed in Japan. I can neither confirm nor deny that the truck is full of beer.

My trip to Vietnam began on the cargo ship the SS Drake Victory, a refurbished victory ship from World War II. The voyage from Leonardo, New Jersey, to Qui Nhon, Vietnam, took me down the Atlantic, through the Panama Canal, and across the Pacific in fifty-six days. The faded jeans and madras shirt you see here are the only clothes I brought when I went to Vietnam, where I expected to be for only three days. By the end of the trip I was, shall we say, rather ripe.

CHAPTER 5

ANCHORED OFF QUI NHON

We hadn't been told where we were going to land, for security reasons. In the early fifteenth century, Qui Nhon had been a stop for the Ming dynasty eunuch Admiral Zheng He when his armada of treasure ships loaded with gems, gold, porcelain, and even giraffes was returning from one of its expeditions commissioned by the Chinese emperor. Nowadays in Qui Nhon, a provincial capital four hundred miles northeast of Saigon, the treasure was oil—it was the primary place where the US military transferred petroleum products from oceangoing vessels to the giant fuel tanks I could see up on the hillside.

What a target for sappers—commandos who'd attach explosives to hulls—the ships were; Tommy Collins's task as a military policeman (MP) was to guard them. Our cargo was to be unloaded by the ship's cranes way out in the harbor onto barges, and we mariners were not to disembark the entire time. I hoped my plan would work, and that the captain would make an exception and let me go ashore.

Now, I usually didn't like captains. I don't like authority figures in general, but captains especially. I didn't speak to them unless it was necessary. The ones I've worked under are usually more like James Cagney's dictatorial Captain Morton in the film *Mister Roberts* than Tom Hanks's noble Captain Richard Phillips in *Captain Phillips*.

Once, when we had delivered cargo to the air force base at Cam Ranh Bay, one of our mariners was sick with jaundice. The captain refused to let him go ashore for treatment. Yet only a few hours later, the captain's Doberman pinscher jumped down the hatch and hurt itself. He immediately had a boat put in the water and commanded two crew members to bring the dog to the medics on the base.

The captain was preparing to go visit his pooch when he called us all on deck.

"I want you to unload all the wood we used to shore up the cargo and load it onto the military trucks at the end of the pier," he ordered gruffly. "After you're finished, don't get any ideas about leaving. I want the hold cleaned spotless after you've emptied it." Then he took off.

The first thing some of us did was take our mate to sick bay at the base.

The next thing we did was unload the fifty spare mattresses we had on our giant ship. I had learned that the young airmen on the base slept on cots, probably tossing and turning in the heat. I explained the situation to my fellow seamen, and, given that we were such a small crew, they all agreed that we should load the Sealy Posturepedics, still in their wrapping, onto the military trucks and cover them with the lumber. The captain wouldn't find out till the ship was back home and its owner discovered the mattresses were missing. By then, we'd be long gone.

In fairness to captains, I wasn't always a teacher's pet, either. It was my custom to have a good time whenever we pulled into port and enjoy what that city had to offer. Isn't that what traveling the world is all about? Admittedly, there had been occasions when I had been brought back to the ship courtesy of a police escort. Like the time in Durban, South Africa, when I was cuffed and arrested by six cops for drinking in a "coloreds-only" club. The dancing in that place was a lot more fun than in Lily White's All-Night Apartheid Hideaway, let me tell you.

This time I wasn't even sure that they would allow us mariners off the ship once we anchored off Vietnam. I'd been in war ports where we offloaded cargo—especially dangerous cargo—by crane onto barges in the middle of the harbor while you gazed longingly at the shore. If that were so, I hoped that, because I was the union chairman, the captain would look the other way. I absolutely had to disembark in Vietnam.

I'd also learned that the only thing that captains give a damn about is that the ship's work gets done. And that nobody bothers them in the process.

Once we anchored off Qui Nhon, I went to the captain. He regarded me warily, since we had barely exchanged a word during the entire journey.

"Captain?"

"What is it, Donohue? I'm very busy here."

"Well, sir, I don't know if you know this, but I have a stepbrother serving here in Vietnam . . ."

"How would I know that?"

"Well, you wouldn't, of course, Captain, but, anyway, we've had terrible news in the family which I feel I have to break to him personally, as he's in a stressful enough situation here and—"

"Are you shitting me, Donohue? You really wanna go to a brothel, am I right?"

"No, no, no, Captain! It really is quite devastating news, and I really have to see my stepbrother face-to-face, or the news might be too much."

I didn't want to actually lie and say, "Our mother has cancer," or something like that and jinx her! And I said "*step-*brother," in case he checked on the last name.

Sure enough, all he cared about was the job.

"What about the engine room?!" he fumed. It still had to be maintained, though we were at anchor. I had traded nine extra shifts with my shipmates to cover my pilgrimage.

"Don't worry, Captain," I said. "My shifts are covered for the next three days."

That's how long I thought my mission would take. I guess I was a little naïve.

He paused for what seemed like an eternity. Finally, he blurted out, "All right, Donohue. But you'd better be back on deck by 0800 hours Monday, you understand?"

"Yes, sir, thank you!"

"In the meantime, Donohue, *don't get killed.* I wouldn't want to do all that paperwork."

CHAPTER 6

LOOKING FOR
CHUCKLES'S BROTHER

If I'd gotten killed onshore, the captain would have had a lot of explaining to do. But I'd been to Vietnam twice before, and back then, it was about as dangerous as the Bronx—you simply avoided certain areas. I thought it would take about two or three days to finish the job.

I went down to the ship's massive refrigerator and dug deep in the back. The beer I had brought from New York was still hidden in there. Nearly a case of good-old American brands would be a nice start. I transferred them into my pack along with a razor and a pair of socks. A taxi boat took me across Qui Nhon Harbor.

The water taxi dropped off some army military police to guard the *Drake Victory*, and now it was ferrying a second contingent of MPs to another cargo ship in the harbor. The MPs in Qui Nhon conducted town patrol and guarded POW camps on land. But they also protected cargo ships, which could be taken over by guys with automatic weapons in sampans—small, sheltered, flat-bottomed boats. Or, as in the case of the USNS *Card*—the "hunter-killer" that had sunk eleven Nazi U-boats in World War II—was itself sunk in Saigon Harbor in 1964 when it suffered a thirty-foot hole blown into it by a single frogman with a sticky bomb, killing five.

I saw that the sides of their helmets bore the distinctive green-and-yellow sword-and-ax insignias of the 127th MP Company. That was Tommy Collins's outfit.

As we pushed off, I asked them, "Do you guys by any chance know Tommy Collins?" Tom Collins was a common name. "Tommy Collins from New York?"

"Yeah, we know Collins," one answered. "As a matter of fact, we're going to relieve him right now. He's on that ship right over there."

They pointed to another American cargo vessel.

Were they pulling my chain? I couldn't be that lucky, could I?

"Well, would you take me over to him?" I asked.

Another answered, "Sure, no problem."

We sped over to the ship, and to paraphrase the poet, what to my wondering eyes did appear but Tommy Collins, standing right there on deck, waiting to be relieved.

"Hey, Collins!" I shouted up. "Tommy!"

Tommy peered down into the boat and did a double take.

"*Chickie?!*" He scurried down the ladder and grabbed me by the arms as if to see if I was real. He looked bigger and stronger than when I'd seen him last, and he was full of questions.

"Chickie! Are you kidding me? How did you get here? Are you nuts? *What the hell are you doing here?!*"

I pulled a beer out of my pack and handed it to him.

"This is from the Colonel and me and all the guys in Doc Fiddler's," I told him. "We all talked about it, and we decided that somebody ought to come over here and buy you guys a drink in appreciation for what you are doing. Well, here I am!"

Then I remembered Mrs. Collins, who had been waiting for me that day at the bar. "Oh, and your mother says you'd better write her so she knows you're okay."

Tommy threw back his head and laughed. He had this quizzical look on his face, as if he were seeing things. As the boat headed into port, I said, "Go ahead, man, open it. It's a cold one!" Tommy popped open the can of beer and chugalugged the entire thing. I guess that was the tonic for his shock because he squinted at me and burst into laughter again.

"What the hell are you wearing, man?" he asked. "White jeans and a madras shirt? You look like you're going on a golf outing!"

Tommy was right: I kind of stood out. I had thrown on clothes I knew would be cool in the ship's engine room, and I hadn't really planned out a travel wardrobe for Vietnam.

The launch reached shore, and I went with Tommy to his base camp. We drove in an open jeep through the bustling town of Qui Nhon. I saw the overgrown ruins of the famous Thap Doi Cham Towers with its gargoyles in the image of Garuda—half bird, half man—carved centuries ago by the Hindus, just one more group that had dominated Vietnam only to be conquered by a Confucian emperor.

Nearby, young women in loose, light-colored martial arts pajamas were executing incredibly acrobatic moves. They were practicing a form of self-defense that trains women to leverage much larger opponents. In another courtyard, men in black pajamas were going through their own self-defense moves, wielding every imaginable weapon, like Bruce Lee: broadswords, spears, rakes, hammers, chain whips—even pitchforks. I was hoping the women didn't have to take on the armed men.

When we got to his barracks, Tommy's bunkmates couldn't believe I had come there to bring him a drink.

"Believe it, guys," I told them, "because I'm buying for you, too." I felt flush with my overtime merchant mariner cash.

They were all off duty now, so we jumped into a couple of jeeps and headed back into Qui Nhon. The road was thronged with bikes and mopeds, and since there were no traffic lights to speak of, the few cars beeped their horns the whole time. We drove through this cacophony to a bar with a clamor of its own. The place, lit with red lamps and strobe lights, featured pretty young women in traditional silk *ao dai* dresses that had been drastically shortened from their usual floor length into miniskirts. They were go-go dancing on the bar to American music playing as loud as a BUFF—a B-52 Stratofortress.

We sat down, and at the sight of six MPs and a mystery man, several of the women moseyed over and sat with us.

"You want to buy us Saigon teas, soldier?" one of them asked Tommy's buddy. Saigon tea was the watered-down Kool-Aid the women sold for four bucks a pop, which they would drink, since the boss wanted them to stay sober. It was your price for having them sit with you. I bought the young ladies Saigon teas, and the guys drank beer and did shots.

The funny thing was, if we were back home, some of them wouldn't have been legally allowed to drink liquor unless they were from New York or Florida or a couple of other southern states. Until they passed the Twenty-Sixth Amendment in 1971, the federal government also considered these young men old enough to die for their country but not old enough to vote.

Before long, they were roaring with laughter when Tommy and I told them how we used to swim naked in the Spuyten Duyvil and moon the sightseers on the Circle Line boats. They, in turn, told us stories about the far-flung towns from which they hailed. In the military, you meet farmers and ghetto guys, surfers and factory workers, teachers and truck drivers, from Detroit to East Hubcap, Idaho. You can't believe we're all from the same country.

The women were flirtatious, but the night wasn't about that. Tommy, the other MPs, and I partied late and closed the bar. We then headed back to base camp and kept the party rolling in the barracks with a "to-go" carton of booze I had purchased from the bartender.

Camped next door were soldiers from the Republic of Korea (ROK) army. South Korea was America's biggest ally, supplying 320,000 troops over the course of the war. Despite the late hour, the ROK guys were outside, working out: more martial arts. They were really into self-defense; in fact, of the first 140 South Korean soldiers sent to Vietnam in '64, 10 were tae kwon do instructors.

Tommy Collins, MP (right), was the first buddy I found, in the port city of Qui Nhon. Tommy's standing with fellow MP Gil Larpenter. I'll never forget the look on Tommy's face when he saw me. "Chickie, what the hell are you doing here?" He would see some intense fighting during the Tet offensive.

We were observing them quietly and sipping our drinks for a while when Tommy said, "Hey, Chickie, let's sing some of the old songs, like we used to in the park."

In Inwood Hill Park, we would sit on the steps and drink beer and sing songs and tell stories and laugh, reaching a magic point of feeling good together among friends that you can't alone. In Ireland, they call it the *craic,* pronounced "*the crack.*"

So, we were doing the same thing here, outside the little barracks, talking and singing the Irish songs:

Ireland was Ireland when England was a pup
Ireland will be Ireland when England's number's up!

And on to:

There was Johnny McEldoo and McGee and me
And a couple of two or three went on a spree one day!
We had a bob or two, which we knew how to blew
And the beer and whiskey flew and we all felt gay!

There were so many verses that even the guys from Mississippi were singing along on the chorus by the end. I guess we were a bit loud, because, all of a sudden, a young lieutenant came out and yelled at Tommy and the others, "*What's going on here, soldiers?!!*"

They snapped to attention as well as they could, but I sat there.

I don't know what possessed me, but I said to him in an authoritative voice, "Lieutenant! On what authority are you questioning these men?! We are on a particular mission here tonight, and I suggest you return to your barracks!"

The lieutenant turned toward me as if he were going to tear me apart. But he suddenly clammed up, turned around, and went back inside.

"What the *hell?!*" Tommy exclaimed.

It was the first of many instances in Vietnam where officers would treat me with the utmost deference, and, at first, I couldn't understand why. Then one day somebody told me:

"Don't you *get it,* pal? They think you're CIA! Because why the hell else would you be here? In jeans and a plaid shirt, no less."

Following their Office of Strategic Services predecessors in World War II, Central Intelligence Agency operatives had been in Vietnam since the early 1950s, when it was still under French rule, a situation Graham Greene depicted in *The Quiet American.* But when the French left after their stunning defeat by North Vietnamese General Vo Nguyen Giap's forces at the Battle of Dien Bien Phu in 1954, CIA agents began a covert operation to turn the Vietnamese against the Communists. It was led by none other than the CIA's master of psychological warfare Edward Lansdale, thought to be the basis of *The Ugly American.* In 1968, CIA agents were still an omnipresent element of the US war effort. I didn't purposely try to impersonate an agent to the officers, but the "CIA Effect" would help me a lot in the coming days.

The boys were tired anyway and would be able to sneak in only a couple hours of rest, so we called it a night. Tommy gave me a sleeping bag, and I spent the night in their barracks. In no time, it seemed, we heard reveille.

I said, "Okay, Tommy, I'm gonna take off. I'm going to go see Rick Duggan up north." The last anybody had heard, Rick was in An Khe, somewhere up in the Central Highlands.

"How the hell are you gonna make it up *there?*"

"Oh, don't worry about that," I said.

He didn't know I'd made arrangements with a Texan who'd been at the bar the night before. "You wanna come along, Tommy?" I asked.

"Well, if I could, sure!" he answered, and he brought me to his sergeant major's office in a Quonset hut.

"Sir," I said, "I am going up to the Central Highlands to find my stepbrother, as I have to deliver important family news to him. Our family friend Thomas Collins here has offered to escort me."

The sergeant major looked me up and down; then he frowned at Tommy.

He turned back to me and growled, "The only thing Collins is going to escort is his own ass back to port, and you can go on your merry way, whatever the hell you're up to. You know, you can't go anywhere in this country without orders. I'll give you a pass, but that's it. You're lucky I'm doing that."

We walked out, and I could tell Tommy was disappointed that we couldn't make it a block party up north with Rick, but he covered with his usual cheer.

"Hey, we gave it a shot, Chickie!"

"Yeah, and we don't want the sappers to find out the best MP in Qui Nhon is off duty."

That made him smile. I gave him a big bear hug and took off down the road. I hitched a ride with a Hanjin Shipping Company truck driver, one of the civilian Korean drivers paid by the United States to run ammo up to our front lines. They were incredibly brave dudes.

"So long, Chickie!" Tommy yelled, and the other guys we'd partied with waved.

"I'll see you back in the neighborhood, Tommy!"

I prayed I would. I felt optimistic, though, because I had found him when I wasn't even looking for him. Whether it was luck or divine intervention, I still don't know, but something good had shined on us.

CHAPTER 7

THE TEXAN COULDN'T CARE LESS ABOUT ORDERS

In the bar in Qui Nhon, Tommy and I had been drinking with a ponderous sergeant from Texas who was wearing a patch on his uniform with a black horse head set against a yellow background—a First Air Cavalry patch. Ricky Duggan was in the First Air Cavalry Division's Bravo Company. The First Cavalry had actually been an US Army horse unit until the middle of World War II, but now the cavalry rode choppers—six hundred of them. Its division had the largest helicopter force in the world.

I had asked the sergeant, "Do you know where Bravo Company is?"

He replied, "Yeah. They're up in the highlands. Why?"

"Well, my stepbrother's up there, and I'm trying to catch up with him."

The Texan drawled, "Well, why don't you come with me? We've got our plane."

I realized the Air Cavalry pilots and crew had their own aircraft and greater independence from their superiors.

He was the crew chief. I told him that when I was in the marines I had flown mostly on Lockheed C-130 Hercules—the huge four-engine prop planes capable of carrying twenty tons of troops or cargo—but I fessed up that I didn't have military orders.

The Texan couldn't care less about orders.

"You can run up with us," he said. "We've got a mail run tomorrow morning. Be at the Qui Nhon airstrip at 0800 hours, and I'll take ya' up there, boy."

Translation: eight o'clock in the morning. That wouldn't be easy after the celebratory reunion with Tommy Collins. Luckily, the Hanjin driver was also running late to deliver cargo to a plane. He floored it all the way.

We arrived at the airstrip in time. There wasn't much there besides rudimentary wooden buildings with corrugated roofs, sandbag bunkers, and some tents. It was a humble backdrop for the magnificent plane shining there: a Grumman Albatross, the trusty flying boat used extensively for search and rescue missions by the air force, army, navy, and coast guard during the Vietnam War. The Texan was standing next to it on the tarmac, and he was even bigger than he had looked on the barstool.

"Goddamn!" he exclaimed. "You made it! Okay, buddy, get on board."

He loaded up a bunch of guys, and I was one of them. I felt incredibly lucky. We took off. It was the first time I had been in a plane over Vietnam. I saw the giant Buddha outside Qui Nhon, gazing out over the troubled land. From up there, the tree-covered hilltops looked so peaceful. But I knew that what was going on in those tangled thickets was anything but.

The Vietnamese novelist Bao Ninh, who fought for the North against our forces, wrote years later in *The Sorrow of War* that the Vietnamese believed the jungle was haunted by the spirits of all the fighters who had died in there—from whichever side.

We flew about forty miles northwest to the Central Highlands and soon landed in An Khe, in Gia Lai Province. I thanked the Texan profusely as I climbed out. Other crew members tossed their mailbags out the door, and the Albatross immediately took off.

I looked around and saw hardly anybody. The First Air Cavalry's Bravo Company was gone.

The few who remained took delivery of the mailbags and told me that their company had decamped early that morning to get closer to the DMZ at the border with North Vietnam. The men of the First Air Cav could fly everywhere in their choppers, so it wasn't as if I could catch up with them on foot or even by jeep. The demilitarized zone was about two hundred miles north, at the 17th parallel; they could be anywhere at this point. According to the soldiers, their supply sergeant and some others were still wrapping things up about a mile up the road. I hiked up there and found the sergeant—probably career army, as he looked to be almost forty.

"Do you know Rick Duggan?" I asked.

"Who wants to know?" he retorted.

"I'm his stepbrother," I said. It wasn't *exactly* true, unless *feeling* like a brother counted. "I have to find him. Do you know him?"

"Yeah."

"He was stationed here?"

"Yes, he was." The sergeant seemed like a guy who had seen it all by the time he was twelve, and a lot of it hadn't looked good.

"Um, do you know where he is now?"

"Duggan and the rest of the company moved up north."

"Where?"

"I don't know where," he answered. "Just *north*."

I *was* truly bummed out, and I guess he could see that. After a minute, he softened and said, "Tell ya what. You can write him a letter, and they can deliver it to him this afternoon."

"You told me you don't even know where he is—but you can get a letter to him this afternoon?"

"Of course!" he yelled, sounding exasperated. "We've got a 1300 mail run going!" He said it like: *"Doesn't everybody know that?!!"*

So, I said, "Hey . . . can *I* get on that 1300 mail run?"

He looked at me deadpan and said, "Well you got *here*, didn't ya?!"

I took that as a yes. It was 1200 hours. There wasn't much time left.

CHAPTER 8

THE GOOD SAMARITAN IN AN KHE LOOKED FAMILIAR

I headed back toward An Khe, hurrying to make it back to the airfield. I was walking alone on a dirt road through the jungle. They had closed the road, and the whole outfit had been moved out, so there wasn't any traffic. In fact, there was nothing: not a shack or any sign of people along the way. When I heard an engine, I spun around and saw a jeep coming my way. I waved it down.

There were three men in the jeep, the driver in civilian coveralls and the other two in military uniform. They stopped ahead of me. The driver said, "Hop in." He didn't even turn around. I jumped in the back.

"We gotta get to the village quick, man," the good Samaritan said as he drove. "But we have a cardinal rule over here: never pass an American. Where're you headed?"

"North," I answered. "I'm lookin' for somebody."

"What?! This is a nice place to be looking for somebody," he remarked.

I started to elaborate, and the guy whipped his head around and screeched to a halt.

"Holy Christ!! Chick!! What the *hell?!!*"

"Kevin?!!!!"

The good Samaritan was my friend Kevin McLoone, who was on my list! I couldn't believe it. I wasn't even looking for him yet!

"*What the hell are you doing here?!*" Kevin asked, on the verge of shock.

"I'm here to find you!" I said. "And Rick, and Bobby, and Tommy and Joey and Rich and the other guys. I brought you some great beer from New York; because the gang wants you to know how much we appreciate you."

The two soldiers in the jeep looked at each other wide eyed, and Kevin shook his head in disbelief. After a few seconds, he said, "Wow! That's a helluva beer run!"

Luckily, I had enough of the local New York brands in my backpack to share with them and still have some left for Rick Duggan and some of the GIs with him, not to mention Bobby and Joey and Rich.

"Okay, Chick," Kevin said. "What do you want me to do?"

I told Kevin I wished I could hang out with him for a while longer, but I'd never find all the guys on my list in time to return to my ship if I did.

"Can you get me to the airstrip as quickly as possible?"

"You got it, buddy," Kevin said, flooring it through the jungle.

I passed out cans to Kevin and his buddies, whom Kevin introduced as Jim and Tony.

"I know they're warm," I apologized.

Kevin McLoone served as one of the first US Marines in Vietnam from 1963 to 1967. Then he went back. He returned as a civilian to scramble the radio signals of choppers so North Vietnamese regulars and Vietcong guerrillas couldn't detect pilot movements.

"Who cares?!" Jim exulted and popped open the can.

"Love that sound," he said as he passed one can to Kevin. Then he opened his and took a long sip with closed eyes. Meanwhile, Tony chose to chugalug.

"Mmmmm. I haven't had Rheingold for a year," Jim noted.

"Dare I drink and drive?" Kevin asked rhetorically as he savored a sip.

Kevin had served four years in Vietnam in the US Marine Corps' HMM-261 helicopter squadron known as the Raging Bulls, starting in 1963 up in Da Nang. President Kennedy was still alive then, and the American presence was on the downlow. The Raging Bulls were the third US Marines unit to arrive in Vietnam—only about 250 men, including pilots. They stayed in an old French Foreign Legion compound in Da Nang with two US Special Forces A-teams—also known as Green Berets—as well as two to three hundred ARVN (Army of the Republic of [South] Vietnam) paratroopers, and the tribal hill people known as the Montagnards.

The Montagnards were fiercely loyal to the US Special Forces, who were training them, even as they were treated like dirt by the South Vietnamese because they were ethnic minorities. Kevin said the Montagnards were still wearing loincloths when he first got there. They sensibly refused to eat C-rations and would hunt monkeys with small crossbows and poison-tipped arrows; or they'd convince a chopper pilot to pick up a pig or some chickens in a basket from their village in the mountains. Even though they were good fighters, every so often the tribal chief would declare that it was their time to drink a wormwood mash out of a communal bowl. It tasted like anisette but had a narcotic effect like absinthe—"like the crazy

French painters used to drink," Kevin said. They'd be out of commission for a couple of days, then it was back to fighting.

My friend had finished his tour the year before, but he'd learned so much about helicopters that now he'd come back with the private contractor Dynalectron as an aircraft electrician to help stop so many from being shot down, resulting in terrible casualties.

"The NVA and the VC were picking up the pilots' radio signals on the FM band," Kevin explained. "It was as if the pilots were announcing their imminent arrival." He and his cohorts were installing signal-scrambling systems on every single chopper radio, eliminating the problem.

The last stretch was up a steep hill, and when we came over the top, I was so happy: the two-engine prop plane doing the 1300 mail run was there. But I couldn't just walk on. Kevin escorted me to the pilot.

"I need to hitch a ride up north," I said to him.

"Fine," he replied. "Go into operations and show them your orders."

"I don't have any orders," I confessed. The pilot sized me up for a minute, then said, "Well, at least go put your name on the manifest"—the flight's list of passengers and crew.

So, I went inside "operations," which basically consisted of a Quonset hut with a GI sitting at a folding table. I addressed him in that authoritative voice that had worked so well with the lieutenant in Qui Nhon:

"You've got a flight going north at 1300 hours?"

"Yes, sir," the GI answered.

"Good," I responded. "Put my name on the manifest: John Donohue. Put down . . ." I paused for effect. "'Civilian.'"

He frowned as he squinted at me; then he nodded and wrote it down.

I went out with Kevin, and about a dozen GIs and two or three officers were waiting. Moments later, a GI with a clipboard arrived and read off the names, calling the officers onboard first. Then he said, "Wait a second. We got a civilian here?"

Gulp.

"Donohue!"

"Yeah!"

"Go ahead, sir, you can board now." You know, like when the airlines board the priority-seating people on the plane first. *Whew.*

I turned to Kevin, who looked me right in the eye and said, "I gotta tell ya, Chick, in all my time here, I haven't met anybody who's not in the military or a civilian with work orders. Even the potheads avoid this place—they're all hanging out in Chiang Mai over in Thailand. But you're the first guy I've encountered who's roaming around Vietnam looking for somebody. Good luck with your search, Chick." We shook hands.

"Thanks, buddy. I'll see ya back home," I said and walked to the plane. As with Tommy, I prayed silently that we *would* meet up again.

I hopped on, followed by all the GIs, and we took off.

CHAPTER 9

LZ TOMBSTONE

I took a seat on one of the benches that run on either side of the fuselage so that the cargo can be loaded in the middle. The plane took off, heading north. I was jazzed. I'd already found two of my guys. I was thinking, *This is going to be a bunt!* I was hoping I would find Rick, and soon. I didn't have much time left.

I was sitting next to two young soldiers. We started talking—yelling, actually—over the din of the engine. They had been wounded and were now returning from the hospital to be sent back into combat.

They didn't ask me any questions.

I asked them, "Do you know where Bravo Company is?"

"Me and my buddy are in Bravo Company," one kid answered.

"I'm looking for a guy in Bravo Company named Rick Duggan."

"He's in our company," the more outgoing GI offered.

"Well, I'm a friend of his from the old neighborhood," I said, "and I've come over here to bring him a beer."

I still had about ten cans of New York's finest left in my pack after the encounter with Kevin McLoone. I had bought some popular American brands at the base in Qui Nhon, which I drank myself. Hey, it was hot over there, and I was thirsty! But I wanted to save the cans I'd brought from home for my buddies.

The two young GIs looked at each other, and the slightly older, friendlier one burst out laughing. He thought it was funny, but the younger guy wanted nothing more to do with me. If he could have bailed out of that plane and onto another one in midair, he would have. He thought I was going to be trouble, but thank God I didn't turn out to be. At least not for him. That I know of.

"Do you guys know where you're headed?"

"No," said the friendly one. "They never tell us."

"Well, I hope you don't mind if I follow you, then."

"Yes, we do mind!" said the wary kid. "We don't want to have anything to do with you! Jack, stop talking to him."

That only made Jack laugh even harder. I wanted to hand *him* a beer. But I don't blame the cautious kid. He couldn't help it. I was still in dungarees and the plaid sports shirt. My hair was getting a little long around the edges. I hadn't had a shower, or shaved, or had a haircut since I disembarked. You might even say I was unkempt.

The suspicious GI looked to be about eighteen years old maximum, and he'd already been wounded and sewn up and was now being sent back to the jungle. He'd probably grown up in a town with more cows than people, and he didn't know what the hell was going on. I hoped he'd make it back to that little town all right.

The plane landed at Phu Bai, a major military airfield on the coast, ten miles south of the old imperial city of Hue.

In 1965 General Westmoreland had ordered a thousand marines to dig and fill thousands of sandbags to establish a camp there. They did so in thirty days. Then the four-star army general, who prior to the Vietnam War had been a highly respected veteran of both World War II and the Korean War, changed his mind and sent many of those marines up to the Con Thien and Cam Lo combat bases, only two and four miles, respectively, from the DMZ. Westmoreland, believing that the main objective of North Vietnam's military leader, General Vo Nguyen Giap, was to seize the northern provinces, had just sent other leathernecks, disastrously, to remote Khe Sanh, against the wishes of the top marine commanders. Westmoreland then expanded the presence of the army into the beachside camp at Phu Bai, and ever after, the marines claimed they had built an Acapulco for the GIs.

We got off the plane, and I followed the two GIs, hanging back maybe twenty, thirty feet. They got into the back of a PC—a personnel carrier—joining two other soldiers. As soon as it started moving, I caught up and ran alongside, then gave it a hit. It screeched to a stop. I hopped in the back, banged it twice, and off we went. Those were the international signals: one for stop, two for go.

All the young GIs were now staring at me except for Jack, who winked at me conspiratorially. As we wended our way north through the hills, it struck me again what a beautiful place Vietnam was—like the Great Smoky Mountains, only hotter. It had huge trees in the forest, even evergreens. Crazy-crowned hoopoe birds, drongos with their bandit masks, and blue-Mohawked kingfishers trilled and zipped among the teak trees as tall as ship masts, and the jackfruit trees laden with fruits that could weigh a hundred pounds. They didn't smell so good, but the fragrant frangipani flowers all along the way made up for it. I felt at peace for one moment—until the scream of a forest eagle owl totally spooked me. It sounded like a woman crying for help somewhere deep in the woods; no wonder the Vietnamese consider an encounter with one to be a bad omen.

We wound up at an old French country church. Nothing was around it but an old cemetery they called Landing Zone Tombstone. There were sixteen, eighteen helicopters, all parked up the hillside. Apparently, they'd arrived only that afternoon.

Jack told me to hitch a ride with them on one of those helicopters to Landing Zone Jane before sunset to catch up with Bravo Company. I knew they would lead me right to Rick; I had to stick with them.

I walked into the operations tent and said casually to the corporal at the table, "Got a chopper going up to LZ Jane at 1800 hours?"

He looked a little perplexed but answered, "Yes, sir!"

"Okay," I said. "Put my name on the manifest."

The GI said, "Um . . . um, what's your rank, sir?"

"I'm a civilian," I said.

"A civilian, sir?" he said. "You really have to speak to the major about this."

The major walked into the tent, talking with another officer. The GI waited to get his attention and then explained the situation.

The major turned to me and said, "You want to go to LZ Jane? Where are you coming from?"

"From down south, sir," I said. "I've got to see someone at LZ Jane."

I wasn't keeping it vague on purpose, but it worked in my favor.

"I see . . ." said the major, and he gave me a knowing look. It was the CIA Effect, working its magic again.

"Okay, right. I understand. Corporal, put Mr. Donohue on the list."

"Did you eat yet?" he asked me, and I said I hadn't. So, the major put his arm around me, led me to the mess tent, and we had dinner together.

During the meal, he told me all about what had been going on up there. I couldn't believe I was sitting there dining with a major. I went into the marines a private, and four years later, I came out a private. But I was a four-star general when it came to slinging BS. At one point, he leaned over and asked furtively, "Can you tell me a little bit about what's going on?"

"Sure, I'd be glad to," I said. "See, I have a stepbrother, Rick, who's in Bravo Company, and I'm going to bring him a beer."

With that, he burst into laughter and shook his head.

"You guys from Saigon are all alike!" he said. "You keep everything to yourselves!"

Then it was 1800 hours—time to go. I thanked the major and headed to the chopper pad.

The two returning GIs and I climbed aboard the chopper, a Bell UH-1 Iroquois—a "Huey"—heavily armed, with guns on both sides. In all my years in the marines, I had been in a helicopter only once, when I was medevacked out of the Vieques Naval Training Range in Puerto Rico after a jeep

Vietnam was the first "helicopter war," with choppers supplanting the need for GIs to parachute into combat zones. Here, soldiers ride open-air in a Bell UH-1 Iroquois ("Huey") gunship mounted with an M60 machine gun.

accident during maneuvers. Medical evacuation was one of the primary uses of choppers at first. Though the US Army bought its first Sikorsky in 1941 and used a chopper for the first time in World War II to rescue downed airmen in Burma three years later, the military relied primarily on paratroopers airdropped from planes to perform such rescues in World War II. In the Korean War, rotary aircraft were used mostly for reconnaissance, supply, or medical evacuation of the wounded, like any fan of the TV show *M*A*S*H* would know. There were a few paratrooper drops in Vietnam—Jimi Hendrix even completed parachute training at Fort Campbell, Kentucky, but never got to Vietnam since he was honorably discharged, because, as one of his commanding officers said, "his mind apparently cannot function while performing duties and thinking about his guitar" at the same time.

But there was only one mass jump: Operation Junction City, involving 845 paratroopers over eighty-two days in 1967 in search of what was thought to be a hidden headquarters of the Vietcong. Meanwhile, there were nearly twelve thousand US helicopters flown by forty thousand pilots, and our allies the Royal Australian Air Force (RAAF) had its own fleet, engaging in combat, landing and taking off from places where only paratroopers could reach before. Vietnam was the first helicopter war.

You fly with the doors wide open, and I have to admit, about halfway to Pleiku, I was scared. We were headed to Hai Lang up in Quang Tri Province, less than an hour from the DMZ. We were not over friendly territory.

Now, a little thing I did not know about choppers is how much the wind rushes inward. And I must confess, I passed gas. The pilots and the GIs made a big deal of it; I guess it was bad.

So, the pilot cut off the engine. He yelled, "Okay, everybody out now! This is unbearable!"

And we started to drop. I thought we were going to crash into enemy territory. I was totally freaking out. Then the pilots looked at each other and started roaring with laughter. They turned the engine back on, and we swooped up. They'd been busting my chops.

CHAPTER 10

"WHO'S *THIS* GUY?!"

By the time we got to LZ Jane in Quang Tri Province, it was early evening. The chopper landed in an open, hilly field. There were no structures in sight, nothing but a windflag to mark a safe landing spot, stuck in the ground. The two GIs and I got out, and—*whoosh!*—the chopper took off and was gone. A sergeant major and some other GIs appeared.

The sergeant major yelled, "Who's *this* guy?!"

The kid who had been wary of me yelped, "I don't know! I don't have anything to do with him! He's been following us!"

The sergeant major was the highest officer in the vicinity. Whoever had the most stripes was in charge. So, I told the guy with a star on his stripes who I was and what I was doing. Luckily, he thought it was hilarious.

"Duggan's out at the ambush post," he said, smirking. He was in on it now.

The sergeant major turned to his radio operator and said, "Hey, call Duggan back in." While the GI worked the field phone, the officer pointed to the ground.

"Get in here, quick."

They had already dug a deep foxhole; a place to take cover under fire. I jumped in, and they threw a poncho over me.

"RV12845, return to the perimeter," I heard the radio operator say. "RV12845, return to the perimeter."

They would always refer to a soldier by his roster number, because if the enemy was listening in and heard his name over the radio, they could use it for propaganda purposes.

I was crouched down, hiding in that hole. The ambush patrol was two hundred yards away, and it would be kind of sketchy for Rick to come back alone. I started to worry I would get him killed, but after a while, I heard his familiar voice. I smiled to myself.

"You called me back in, sir?" Rick asked. "You wanted to see me?"

"Oh, *we* don't want to see you," the sergeant said. "*This guy over here* wants to see you."

Presto! They yanked the canvas off the top of the hootch, and out I jumped.

Rick did a double take and turned and looked over his shoulder for coconspirators—there were none.

"*Chickie! Holy s—! What the hell are you doing here?!*'"

"Here's a beer for you," I said, and I explained my mission.

"*Are you kidding me?!*" he said. "No, really, come on, what are you doing here?"

"That's really what I'm doing here," I said.

The sergeant and the other guys were laughing hysterically.

"But who are you with?" Rick asked. He looked like he was still processing it; like I was a mirage.

"Who am I with?" I said. "I am with you!"

Then the sergeant major said, "Duggan, you'd better get the

hell out of here because he's not supposed to be here. I know that much."

"What do I do with him?" Rick asked him.

"He's yours now—take him with you," the officer declared.

*Here is Rick with his buddy "T-Bo" Tobias, who often
volunteered to be point man on patrol. As I sipped the
beer with Rick and his fellow soldiers, one of them said
to me, "Wait a minute. You're telling me you don't have
to be here, and you're here?!"*

CHAPTER 11

"WAIT A MINUTE—YOU DON'T HAVE TO BE HERE, AND YOU'RE HERE?!"

Rick looked me over and said, "Here, put my poncho on. That outfit is like wearing a sign that says, 'Shoot me, I'm from New York.'"

Rick looked more bulked up than when I saw him last, having engaged in dozens of combat missions already. He had political ties back home that could have gotten him a desk job, but he hadn't pulled any of them.

By now, it was twilight. I was looking around for a small building, anything—but there was nothing. I had no idea where we were headed, and it didn't feel good.

We went out beyond the perimeter. Picture a large circle, with all the troops inside. There was no fence. About two hundred yards out, on the forward perimeter, were a dozen or so guys. They would sit out there all night as lookouts, so that if anybody was coming in to attack, they would hit them first.

When we arrived at the forward perimeter, one of the GIs appeared taken aback. "Who the hell is this?" he asked.

"Believe it or not," said Rick, "he's from my neighborhood."

They looked at each other, then back at me, and then another soldier said, "Wait a minute—you're telling me you don't have to be here, and you're here?!"

"You mean, did he recently escape from the asylum?" Rick said. "No, he just came to show us support."

They looked at one another again.

"Better yet, he brought us some beer," Rick added.

"Yeah!" more than one of them said.

"That's the good news. The bad news is you can't have it on ambush patrol. You have to wait till tomorrow. And that's an order."

They accepted it without a peep.

The GIs were peppering me with questions about what was going on back home. Is Vince Lombardi really going to retire from coaching football? How short are the girls' skirts now? Do you think they'll have another Summer of Love this year? Are people still rioting? Are they still protesting? Did the Airplane come out with another album? Does everybody have a color TV now? Have you gotten to drive a Mustang? And, the big one: Do you think the war will be over soon?

I answered as best I could.

The stories went on past dark. They were telling us tales from wherever they called home, everything from two-headed sheep, to sharks biting surfboards, to low-rider cars, and we were telling them stories about New York City.

"Is it really true what Duggan told us: that a guy in your neighborhood drove his Volkswagen into a bar and then out the side doors?"

"It was a bar-restaurant and yep, it's true. Pete McGee—through Bickford's, where they have swinging double doors on two sides. He got breakfast to go."

"Is it true that you guys would dive off ninety-foot cliffs in some city river, and you'd have to swim home fast or else get caught in the sewage when they released it right into the river?"

"Spuyten Duyvil Creek, yep."

"Wow," said the kid. "Duggan, no disrespect, but we were always skeptical of your stories before. We believe you now." I think, for a few minutes, they forgot they were in the middle of a war.

At this point, I was pretty exhausted. "Where do I sleep?" I asked Rick.

"In the foxhole, with me and him," Rick answered, indicating one of the younger GIs. "We sleep on the ground."

The other GIs split up into groups and hopped into various foxholes.

One guy had an air mattress in his pack that he blew up for me, which I really appreciated. Then another guy, from Detroit, handed me a .45 pistol.

"What am I supposed to do with this?"

"Well, if we're overrun, try to use it on the enemy—or, if you have to, yourself," the guy said. "Use your judgment."

Great! Use my judgment. I gave it back. I was four years out of the marines, and I was more afraid of shooting one of the soldiers. I was shot once, by accident, when my friend

Foxy Moran and I were teenagers and fighting over a rifle in the park, and I wouldn't wish that on anyone.

But now the guy had awakened me to the reality around us, and as they decided who would take turns sleeping for a couple of hours, I couldn't even close my eyes. Rick got the first turn, and I asked, "How the hell are you going to be able to fall asleep?"

"Well, when it's your turn to sleep, you have to sleep, period," Rick explained. "You hike seven, eight miles a day through thick jungle, and then you dig a foxhole, and come nighttime, you've got to sleep. Because there's nothing between you and the enemy but mosquitoes. And leeches. And the monsoon."

The other guys chuckled, but within a couple of minutes, Rick was there on the ground, out like a light. But I was up like an owl.

CHAPTER 12

FIREFIGHT AT THE
AMBUSH POST

In the middle of the night, one of the guys crawled over to Rick, shook him, and whispered:

"Duggan! Duggan! Where's the Starlight scope?"

Starlight scopes provided a soldier night vision by amplifying moonlight, available starlight, and even sky glow up to thirty thousand times. They were expensive—I think each one cost the army about two grand—and often only one soldier in a squad might have one.

Rick mumbled unintelligibly, and the GI whispered urgently:

"Duggan, please wake up! We need the Starlight scope!"

"You guys are always seeing things," Rick mumbled, and he turned over. "Lemme sleep."

"No, you don't understand, sir!" the GI half-whispered, half-yelled. *"We have movement on the perimeter!"*

Rick snapped awake and hurriedly got out the scope.

The GI took it and hoisted it onto his shoulder—it was a

heavy thing for Rick to carry around all the time—and peered through it toward the jungle.

Rick whispered to me, "The NVA are out there, moving around."

He tried to make light of it, like, oh, it's no problem, it happens every night. He tried to reassure me by saying, "They're probably just passing by. But if they try to overrun us, and we have to pull back, boogie back to our line." He pointed into the darkness behind us across an open field. "Yeah, boogie back over there. Don't worry, Chick, I'll tell you when," he said. "And take this."

Rick handed me an M79—a grenade launcher—the only other weapon he had besides his rifle. So now it seemed the NVA were crawling by us or, worse yet, up to us. They were not on my list of guys to find. I was wondering if my visit might have been a dumb thing to do.

The guy with the scope looked where they thought they saw movement.

"It's NVA," he confirmed.

Rick told the radio operator to call back inside the base perimeter to request illumination.

Within a minute, *Bop! Whizzz!* We heard the flares leave the mortar and fly through the sky. But instead of it going over us and lighting up the sky above the enemy, the first one landed right on top of us: *Bop!* Thank God it never exploded, or it might have lit up our location.

The next one went farther and burst overhead and lit up at least four NVA soldiers in their shallow helmets at the edge of the jungle.

"There they are," said Rick.

The NVA started firing machine guns. Our guys returned fire. I kept really low in that hootch, and I was getting ready to run across that field. The firefight went on and on.

After a while, things went quiet. The GI with the Starlight scope looked through it again.

"Nothing moving," he said.

"You all right, man?" Rick asked me. He looked worried.

"Yeah, I'm okay, thanks," I said. I have to admit, I was shaken. Everybody was up and on alert for the rest of the night, no doubt praying for daybreak. Finally, dawn came, and Rick and his squad headed out with rifles drawn on the jungle. After a few minutes, they returned and picked me up. I don't know what they saw out there, but we ambled back inside the base perimeter in silence. They were preoccupied; there was no conversation and no drama. They'd already seen a lot of action in First Cav, and Rick would see a lot more: 153 combat assaults in all. The month before, he had been in a Central Highlands firefight that lasted six days. An entire North Vietnamese regiment had surrounded them, soldiers armed with Russian and Chinese machine guns that shot a thousand rounds per minute. Rick's company of a hundred soldiers lost twenty-five men, including his platoon commander. My friend had suffered a shrapnel wound during the battle; it was treated in the field. Now he and his buddies were up near the DMZ at the Ben Hai River, right up against the border of North Vietnam.

I tried to keep things normal. "What's for breakfast?" I asked Rick.

Unfortunately, his answer was C-rations: one can of lima beans and another of meatballs. He handed me a P-38 can

Rick kept and carried all his letters from home, as well as certain editions of the military newspaper Stars and Stripes, *in the eighty-five-pound pack he carried for the duration of the war.*

opener—so named because the small, simple tool took thirty-eight turns for it to open a can. Rick also gave me a metal canteen cup with an instant coffee packet so that I could heat up some water and add it. Fine dining, Vietnam style.

While I ate, German shepherd and Doberman guard dogs came up to me, barking. Dogs always barked at me in Vietnam because I stood out; everyone else was in camouflage. I didn't blame them. They were doing what they had been trained to do. The dogs thought I was the enemy.

Rick's pack must have weighed sixty pounds, yet he carried around every letter his mother and grandmother had written to him, as well as every issue of the *Inwood Newsletter*, which a team of seven young women in the neighborhood sent out monthly to all the local guys serving in Vietnam. The newsletters told who got engaged to whom, which softball team was in first place, poems like "Loving a Soldier," bar-naming contests, and calls for essays on topics such as "All Roads Lead to Inwood." They reported that the Inwood contingent in the annual May 1 Loyalty Day parade down Fifth Avenue had six hundred people in it.

Reading one edition, I could see the Colonel was up to his old tricks. He "wanted to send you a bottle of scotch, but it wouldn't fit in the envelope," the ladies wrote. Instead, he'd soaked dozens of bar coasters in booze and had them included with the newsletter along with instructions to "apply it to your tongue every two hours."

Inside the fence, more officers were around. So now I had to explain to the army what I was doing there. I did, and each would give me a "Yeah, right" scowl and go on to his business. They assumed I was an agent on some sort of undercover mission. Back then, there was no way for them to check on that kind of stuff out in the field.

I wasn't important enough to be reported to Saigon. And they were more than a little preoccupied. They announced to the men that they would be moving out the next day to the A Shau Valley west of Hue in Thua Thien Province in South Vietnam. It was a key strategic point for the North Vietnamese army because it was close to the border with Laos, where the NVA threaded down the Ho Chi Minh Trail, named for their president and revolutionary leader, with artillery, weapons, ammo, and other supplies, bursting out into South Vietnam to do battle with our troops. The two long, narrow countries—like California, but smaller—shared a 1,300-mile border and it was porous—ditto farther south along the trail in Cambodia.

US forces hadn't been to the A Shau Valley since 1966, when four battalions of the North Vietnamese army—at least two thousand soldiers—surrounded a Special Forces camp guarded by about two hundred South Vietnamese civilian irregulars, a small company of Montagnards, and seventeen members of the army's elite Special Forces, known more commonly then as the Green Berets. All seventeen Green Berets were casualties, with five killed and twelve wounded, including 2014 Medal of Honor recipient Sergeant Major Bennie G. Adkins, who suffered eighteen wounds while being the last American to defend the camp. What a shit show that was.

Rick and his squad took the news without complaint. They simply went out on patrol, carrying their M16 automatic rifles, and I went with them. We hiked for quite a ways, and, luckily, didn't encounter any more visitors. There were steppes of rice paddies in an iridescent, parakeet shade of green. I commented to Rick, "This looks like Ireland." It was hot, and we stopped for a minute under a tree to sip water from a canteen. I was about to sit down on a boulder when Rick blurted out, "No, Chick! Don't sit on that! That's a baked pile of elephant shit! The NVA use elephants to carry their artillery!"

Here we were fighting soldiers who were half starved, using methods Hannibal had employed two thousand years before, and they were giving us a run for our money. President Johnson and Defense Secretary Robert McNamara were making similar observations in the White House. It would all come out after McNamara quit a month later and LBJ refused to run for reelection the month after that. They quit, but they left our troops behind.

We didn't encounter anybody out there, so we returned to the base perimeter, and Rick and his squad made their report. I was standing near the radio operator, who had to lug around the huge piece of equipment—and he was with the translator—an American of Vietnamese descent who had enlisted. A young GI sat on the ground next to him listening. Over the radio came voices speaking Vietnamese.

The younger GI said, "Who the hell is that?"

The translator answered, "It's the NVA."

"Well, what are they saying?" the kid asked nervously.

"They're talking about supplies."

The kid became irate, yelling, "What the hell are they doing on our radio?!"

"It's not *our* radio, man," the translator snapped. "It's the airwaves, you know?—the air that we share—so shut up so I can hear where they're headed with the damn elephants!"

Armed Vietnamese fighters on both sides of the war used elephants to transport their artillery.

Duggan and the other guys were cleaning their guns and repairing their boots and otherwise preparing to head into the unknown. Then we were back to sitting around telling more stories. Suddenly Rick asked me, "Did you really bring beer? Because I think it would be right on time about now."

I reached into my pack and pulled out all the cans I had except for two and passed them out.

"Here," I said. "Have a warm one."

They popped the cans open and, to a man, closed their eyes as they took their first sip of beer in a while. Maybe they saw their girlfriends. Or a beach back home.

"Mmmm. Warm, but good," sighed Rick.

We told more stories into the night, and then, since other soldiers were on ambush patrol, we all fell asleep right there in the field. Rick used his helmet for a pillow.

Come dawn, we were awakened by choppers, dogs barking, and a cacophony of bird calls. There was already a lot of activity inside the perimeter, and we all got up. At least there hadn't been any attacks during the night.

Rick took me aside and said intently, "Listen, Chick, we're moving out today. And you can't come with us. You don't *want* to come with us, trust me. Let's be serious here. You can't be the company mascot."

He was right, of course. I couldn't help them in what they had to do, though I wished I could. I was worried about them. But I had to find the other guys on my list and catch up with my ship, and I was running out of time.

"We've got to find you a chopper," my friend said.

I said good-bye to the other GIs and wished them luck. I hoped I had brought them some. Rick and I walked to the landing strip, where a big Boeing CH-47 Chinook landed. They were taking a lot of equipment and a jeep off it.

Rick approached a warrant officer and asked, "Do you by any chance have a chopper leaving here and going south?"

"This one's leaving as soon as we empty it, but it's headed east, to the Quang Tri Airfield."

Rick turned to me. "Beggars can't be choosy, Chick."

"Thanks, man," I said. "It's a start. Don't worry."

We went to the pilot, who was in the chopper, and Rick told him, "I've got a civilian here, and I gotta get him outta here pronto. Can you give him a ride?"

The pilot said, "Sure," and waved to me to jump on.

"Well, I guess this is it," Rick said. "I don't mean to give you the bum's rush, man. The fact that you showed up is, like, Whoa, there are actually people back home who care about us!"

We shook hands, and I said a little prayer for him in my head. I waved at him from the door and yelled over the chopper's din, "Okay, Rick! I'll see ya back in the neighborhood!" Rick laughed and gave me a thumbs-up as the Chinook took off.

I dug into some delectable C-rations in Quang Tri Province near the DMZ border with North Vietnam after finding Rick Duggan. Here I am (far right) with Rick (third from left) along with members of his platoon in the First Air Cavalry's Bravo Company.

When I left Rick, I was the solo passenger on the huge Chinook, which could go 196 miles per hour with an 8,000-pound load. It was like flying in an airborne warehouse.

CHAPTER 13

SCREAMS ON THE NIGHT ROAD

I was the only passenger in the cavernous tandem-rotor Chinook. This Boeing-built workhorse could fly 196 miles per hour at high altitudes and in ninety-five-degree heat, and could carry a 4,500-ton payload, either inside or via external hoists and hooks. It transported artillery and a jeep to Rick's unit like they were Matchbox toys; and one was later rumored to have airlifted 147 refugees out of Saigon on the day of its fall, in April 1975.

The Chinook landed in an open field.

The pilot said, "This is as close as we can take you."

It was a farm field. No base, no nothing, except for an occasional pile of sandbags. I was on edge, but I understood. One of the duties of pilots was to protect these choppers, which cost the government millions of dollars. Besides, he had work to do, and he hovered for a minute and pointed down the road before he went off to do it. Then he shot straight up in the air about a hundred feet and took off.

I hoped I could board another chopper or plane at the air-field. My captain had told me to be back in three days, and I had already been gone four. While I wished I had been able to spend even more time with Tommy, Kevin, and Rick, I hadn't even found the other guys yet. I hurried in the direction the pilot had pointed: east. Soon enough, I heard a motor in the distance headed my way. It was a jeep with two marines in it. I stuck out my thumb, and they slowed and looked me over but didn't stop—I was really dirty from being out in the field for a couple of days.

They kept going, and I yelled after them, "Hey! Are you guys headed to Quang Tri Airfield? I need a lift!"

They screeched to a halt. "You speak English?!" one of them asked in astonishment.

I said, "Of course I speak English! I'm from *New York!*"

The driver said, "Sorry, man, we thought you might be a French *colon* who forgot to get the hell outta Vietnam. Hop in." So-called *colons* were French expats in Vietnam left over from the colonial era.

I did, and in a couple of minutes we arrived at the airfield.

I could see a plane on the airstrip, fenced off with barbed wire, and two marines at the gate. One of them held up his arm to stop the jeep. He took one look at me and said, "Can I see your ID, sir?"

The two guys in the jeep sensed a hassle coming. One said, "Look, we gotta deliver these mailbags to that plane."

The marine—he was a corporal—said to me, "Can you step out of the vehicle please, sir?"

I did, and he waved the jeep in, and off they went. I showed him my merchant seaman ID and mentioned that I had been a marine for four years. I could remember my serial number and my rifle number. I still do, and as do most leathernecks. No matter: it was of no help with this kid.

"You are currently a civilian, sir?"

"Guilty as charged."

"I'm sorry, sir. We have orders not to allow any civilians through the gate."

"I think your commanding officer probably meant Vietnamese civilians. Do I look Vietnamese to you?"

"He didn't specify, sir."

"I don't think he was expecting me."

"No, sir."

I wrangled with the corporal for about ten minutes, convinced that the plane was about to take off and that I would be left there another night. I snapped into my newfound voice of authority:

"Call the OD," I barked, meaning the officer of the day. "I need to speak to him. I *must* get on that plane. I'm going over to that operations tent, and I'm going to be taking the next flight out of here."

With that, I started to walk toward the tent.

"Halt!" the corporal shouted. Truthfully, I wasn't sure he wouldn't shoot me. After all, he was a marine. His orders were to stop any civilians trying to enter the airfield, and he was taking those orders literally. He ordered the other marine, a private, to follow me with his M16 pointed at me all the way to the tent, as if I were his prisoner. We got there, with me unventilated—at least for the time being. I went up to the marine sergeant inside, and he informed me it was the last flight out that day.

"Where's it going?" I asked.

"Phu Cat," he answered.

I didn't have to ask if that was south—if we were any farther north, I'd be in Hanoi sitting on Ho Chi Minh's lap.

"Can I grab a seat?" I asked.

He checked my ID, looked me in the eyes, and said, "Sure. Why not?"

He didn't give me a hard time like the corporal had, but I have to say, as a former marine, I was proud of how strictly the kid had followed his orders.

I boarded the plane as it was about to take off.

The sun had set by the time we landed at Phu Cat. It was a major air base built by the United States, with protection from the ROK army's Tiger Division. The VC had constantly harassed the process, setting booby traps by night and shooting at the soldiers and workers with sniper fire by day. Guys died building it, and now, like a lot of military infrastructure we built in Vietnam, it's in civilian use. It is one of the country's most beautiful, modern airports, but at that time, it was home to the 37th Tactical Fighter Wing.

Phu Cat was located seventeen miles northwest of Qui Nhon, where my ship the *Drake Victory* was anchored, and where I had to hustle to, full mission accomplished or not. It was dark out, but I started down the road.

"Where the hell are you going?!" yelled an officer who was overseeing the GIs as they unloaded the plane.

"Qui Nhon," I said.

"Qui Nhon?! You can't make it there tonight! Sign in at the barracks, and they'll give you a bunk."

So, I got a bunk, but there was no way I could sleep. I had

already missed my captain's ultimatum that I be back Monday for my shift—it was Tuesday night. Not only was I in trouble with him, but also I now feared that the ship would depart without me.

I decided to head to Qui Nhon anyway. At the gate, I hitched a ride with another Hanjin truck driver. However, after only about a mile, we came to a fork in the road, and he was not choosing the one less traveled, as I was. I hopped out and started walking, hoping for another truck to rumble up.

I followed the dirt road about a mile into the woods. It was pitch dark except for glimpses of the quarter moon above. There wasn't a jeep or a truck coming from either direction. Something hooted, and I nearly jumped out of my skin. In another half mile, in the middle of the road, a little kid about five years old was bouncing a ball in the dark, throwing it down and catching it over and over. He was all alone, and I said a friendly "*Xin chao*"—"Hello." The kid didn't say anything. He just stood there and stared at me, when I heard a bloodcurdling scream and a torrent of words in Vietnamese.

His mother came running like hell toward us. She looked at me for a split second as she scooped up her kid, turned, and ran toward a little house. I will never forget the look of terror on her face—and the fact that I had caused it.

The officer hadn't cautioned me about the distance to Qui Nhon; he was worried about whom I might encounter along the way. I realized I might be in trouble here. I'd already been wondering whether this was VC territory, and now I was sure. I'd be dumb as a shoe to keep heading toward Qui Nhon on this road in the thick of night, but at this point, I wasn't sure about heading back to Phu Cat, either. Then, by the

In the middle of a war zone you could find the most peaceful and beautiful scenes.

grace of God, out of nowhere, a personnel carrier trundled up. It was empty, except for another old Hanjin driver. These guys sure had stones driving where they did.

The man didn't speak English; I tried my Japanese on him, and he understood some of that. Finally, I asked, "Phu Cat?" and he said, *"Daijobu."* Okay. And I answered, *"Arigatō."* Thank you.

That guy drove me all the way to the gate, overshooting his own destination—one of the many random acts of kindness I would be shown by Koreans and other strangers in Vietnam who helped me on my way.

The guard at the gate asked me, "Where the hell are you coming from?"

"Don't you remember me?" I replied. "I left here earlier. I was trying to find a way to Qui Nhon tonight."

"Are you nuts?! *Charlie's* got that road at night!" he snapped, using the nickname for the VC, short for Victor Charles.

I headed to the barracks and slept fitfully, and at the first hint of sunrise, I hit the road again. A convoy was headed straight to Qui Nhon, and one of the drivers let me ride along in the cab. We went right down the road I'd been on the night before, and I thought, *I was nuts, yeah.* By light of day, I could see all kinds of spots where I could have been grabbed: little wooden bridges, sandbag bunkers—and I would have been gone. I've often thought of that road. If I had been taken and lived, I could have spent the next five years as a prisoner of war. Or worse. When I saw the POWs coming off the planes after the close of hostilities in 1973, I was grateful for how lucky I had been that night.

Qui Nhon was bustling. I didn't have time to return to Tommy's barracks, but I kept my eye out for him on the streets. I didn't spot him, though. The convoy was headed through town all the way to the port, which was lucky for me. What was not lucky for me was this: my ship was gone.

CHAPTER 14

AN AIR FORCE PILOT
DOES ME A FAVOR

I went to the US Coast Guard harbormaster, known to be a no-nonsense dude, and I could see why. The coast guard was tasked with the security of Vietnam's two thousand miles of coastline. Eight thousand Coast Guardsmen served on twenty-six 82-foot patrol boats, cruised more than four million miles, and inspected more than 280,000 vessels over the course of the war. The year before, five high-endurance coast guard cutters, including the USCGC *Winona* and the USCGC *Minnetonka*, had sailed in from Pearl Harbor, Hawaii, destined to engage in six thousand combat missions during the war.

I told the harbormaster I was an oiler on the SS *Drake Victory* and that I had been on a pass to go see my stepbrother. And now the ship was nowhere to be seen in the harbor. I was stuck on the beach, as they say in merchant marine lingo.

He explained that the captain had learned of a possible attack, so he decided to expedite the unloading and get the hell out of there. Normally it would take about six days to un-load cargo like that, but they had sped it up and shipped off. They were sailing back to the States—next stop Manila, the Philippines—and the captain had reported me missing.

"Well, as you can see, I'm not missing," I said.

"You didn't expect them to wait for ya, did you?" he said sharply. Of course not. The worst thing you could do as a sea-man was to miss your ship. Especially in wartime.

I was so disappointed that I wouldn't be able to track down the other guys on my list, especially one of my best friends, Bobby Pappas, who was 375 miles southwest, in Long Binh. But ships don't make U-turns, and now I had to try to catch up with mine.

"All right, look," the harbormaster said. "Maybe you can catch up with the ship. I'll call down to Saigon for them to send you orders to fly there for a visa to leave the country."

That sounded complicated.

"Why don't I go down to Saigon right now?" I asked him.

"You can't go anywhere in Vietnam without orders!" he yelled.

I'd been doing exactly that for nearly a week.

"Tell you what," I ventured, "I'll go down to the US embassy in Saigon now and try to hurry this process up a bit. If the captain didn't wait for me here, he's not going to wait for me in the Philippines."

"Look, I told you, you won't be able to make it to Saigon from here. When you come to your senses, give this to the of-ficer of the day at the barracks, and he'll assign you a bunk."

With that, the harbormaster gave me a signed document. I thanked him profusely and left. But instead of going to the barracks, I left to find Tommy Collins again at his base. I lucked out with him again—he had just come in from guard duty.

"You're back!" Tommy said.

"Yeah, and I'm glad to see you again, but I can't stay. I missed my ship."

"Oh, no!"

"Yeah, and I need to make it down to Saigon ASAP so I can get a military flight out to Manila and catch up with it there."

"Sounds like a plan! What can I do to help?"

"Nothing, man. I wanted to say hi on my way out. This is my mess; I have to undo it. I took too long up north."

"How'd you make out up there? How's Rick?"

"He's doing all right. But while I was up there, we got into a firefight. I saw Kevin McLoone near there, too. They're both in a tough spot up there."

"Wow, you hit a triple, finding three of us already! But I hate to think of you in a firefight, Chickie. Especially in that outfit." He paused, laughing. "Listen, do you want to wash your clothes—and yourself—while you're here?"

I knew I was a little ripe, but there wasn't time.

"I gotta hustle to the airfield now, Tommy. The four of us and Bobby and Joey will all raise a glass to peace back home before you know it!" I gave him a handshake-hug combo, told him again to write to his mother, and took off.

I hurried out to the Qui Nhon airfield. That was the strip where the First Air Cavalry Texan had given me a lift up to An Khe to meet Rick. Maybe, I thought, I could hitch a flight south this time.

The airfield was busier than when I'd been there the other morning, loaded with Hueys, Chinooks, and a few prop planes. I was hoping one of them was about to take off for Saigon—with me on it. I said to an airman with a clipboard at a table in an open tent: "Have you got anything headed south? I need to make it to Saigon as soon as possible. To the embassy."

Big mistake. Mentioning the embassy raised eyebrows.

"Can I see your orders, sir?" the airman asked as others listened in.

"I don't have any orders," I said.

See, the First Cav pilot I'd met in the bar had his own plane. He could do what he wanted. Now, I was back in Bureaucracyland.

"I'm a merchant mariner," I added.

The airman was suspicious, even though in coastal towns during the war, you would see more of a mix: more US Navy sailors, South Vietnamese, Koreans, Aussies, civilian technicians, a few old French *colons*, maybe some European businessmen. But why the hell did a merchant seaman—a filthy-dirty one, no less—need to take a plane?

"A bit far from your ship, aren't you, sir?"

"Exactly. I'm trying to catch up with it."

"I can't put you on one of our aircraft without orders, sir."

I wanted to yell, "*Why the hell not?!*" but my eyelids dropped; I took a deep breath, left the tent, and started to look around. There was another tent at the end of the runway with a lot of activity—guys going in and out. They were wearing the orange coveralls of pilots or crew. I went up to the warrant officer with US Air Force insignia on his collar checking stuff off on a clipboard. When in doubt, find the guy with the clipboard. He was grey haired and looked like he'd been through the realms of hell. I asked him if he had anything headed to Saigon.

He looked at me quizzically. "Yeah," he replied. "Who are you?"

"I'm a merchant seaman," I said, "and I was up seeing my brother. My ship is down in Saigon, and I've got to connect with it before it leaves port"

"Are you s—ing me?" he asked.

Not on the important stuff, I thought.

"No, sir, I am not," I answered.

"Where the hell did you visit him, the mud flats? Look at yourself!"

I was a bit untidy. I knew I wasn't making a good first impression.

"Give me a minute," he said to me, and he went inside the tent.

The officer must have been doing some work in there for a while, but I waited. I think he felt sorry for me, because when he finally came out, he pulled me aside and said conspiratorially, "You see that plane over there?"

It was a gleaming twin-engine Beechcraft Duke, like the ones rich people take out for joyrides.

"Yeah," I responded. "It's a beauty."

"That's my aircraft," he said quietly. "I want you to stand here, and when I board the plane, if I give you a hand signal, don't say a word; go up the steps and in the door and sit in the last seat. Don't talk to any of the passengers, either."

"Okay, man, thanks a lot. I appreciate it," I said.

Three air force pilots boarded, followed by a contingent of official-looking civilians. The Beechcraft pilot walked up the steps, and he turned and gave me the high sign. I jumped on the plane. I buckled myself in. He shut the door, fired up the engine, taxied down the runway, and took right off. The pilot was saving my ass: the flight would take a little over an hour; if I had tried to go by road, it would've been at least twelve hours, with little chance of catching up with my ship.

We flew near the Cambodian border for a while, and I wondered if the VC were hiding in those beautiful tree-covered hills crisscrossed with streams. It reminded me of New York's Catskills Mountains. I was still thinking of home when I was jolted out of my daydream. The pilot had let his copilot take over and he'd come back to the cabin to talk with his fellow pilots, then to make small talk with the other passengers, who turned out to be clergy. Then he headed straight toward me.

He leaned down and said in a hoarse whisper, "If I hadn't been a merchant seaman in World War II, I would've left your rotten ass back there on the tarmac."

"Wow, thanks a lot, brother!" I said.

"When you get to Saigon, do me a favor."

"Name it."

"Take a bath."

CHAPTER 15

STUCK IN SAIGON

When we landed in Saigon, I thanked the pilot again and headed straight for the American consulate. I didn't have time for ablutions, so I rode an army vehicle into the densely packed, bustling city of 1.8 million people.

The South Vietnamese capital was as crowded as Manhattan, with Tu Do Street, aka Independence Street, its Times Square. But instead of yellow cabs, you'd see bikes, motorized or not, and every combination of humanity and the animal world balanced on them: guys with rifles over their shoulders, like war commuters; mothers with two kids and a baby; and men and women transporting all manner of goods on the handle-bars, including ladders, chickens in crates, crab traps, and huge baskets of vegetables.

They'd whiz by older women whose teeth were stained reddish-brown from chewing betel nuts; people selling meat spread out on mats on the sidewalk with dogs running by; Buddhist monks in saffron robes hustling to their temples; vendors selling everything from songbirds to coffins. There was a beautiful temple with dragon boats and other seafaring symbols atop it, maybe dedicated to an ancient sea goddess; I wished I had time to go inside, but I didn't.

The brand-new American embassy and its consulate, built on palm-lined Thong Nhut Boulevard, stood next to the French embassy and across the street from that of the British. After a car-bombing three years before at the old embassy on Ham Nghi Boulevard that killed twenty-three people, including a twenty-one-year-old woman working for the CIA, the United States built a modern, six-storied, fortresslike building that looked impenetrable. All it lacked was a moat.

Once inside, I was shuttled from desk to desk until I finally got to someone who would talk to me. Not only did he talk to me—he already had a missing persons file on me! It said that the captain had been contacted by the coast guard in Qui Nhon and that he'd informed them that he would accept me back on the ship if I could catch up with it. But the embassy official didn't share my sense of urgency about the situation, and in my head, I was soon calling him "Heller," in honor of Joseph Heller, the author of *Catch-22*, the satirical novel about the absurdity of war and the bureaucracy of the military.

"Passport, please."

"I have my seaman's documents. I don't have a passport. I've *never* had a passport—and I've been around the world three times."

"That's nice, Mr. Donohue, but we are in Vietnam in the middle of a war right now, in case you haven't noticed. You need a visa from the Vietnamese government to leave Vietnam, and you need a US passport to obtain a Vietnamese visa."

"Wait—I need a visa to *leave*? Don't most countries require a visa to *enter*? They're probably trying to stop the exodus of their own people trying to get the hell out of here."

"We are guests in their country, Mr. Donohue, and ours is not to question why. Our staff can issue you a passport at the consulate next door."

"Oh, that's good!"

"But not today. Or tomorrow. Maybe not all week. You'll have to have your photo taken and fill out all the forms, and they will be processed, and you will be checked out. When and if you receive your passport, then we can assist you in moving on to the visa process."

"You've just told me that my captain will let me back on ship if I can catch up with it. How am I supposed to catch up with it if I'm sitting here dotting i's and crossing t's on your forms?"

"Sorry, fella, this process will take days," Heller responded. "We're a little busy here."

He was not without pity, though.

"How much money do you have?"

I took out the Vietnamese *piastres* from my pocket and counted them. "About five bucks," I answered.

"Wait a minute," he said. He filled out another form and riffled through his desk till he found a business card.

"Here, contact this guy," Heller said, handing me the card and the form. "He's the agent for the shipping companies that work with the military. Give him this confirmation from us that you're not making up this story, however preposterous. You're going to need food; you're going to need a place to stay; you need money. We're not operating a home for wayward seamen here."

"How long will this process take?!" I asked.

"*A while*," he said brusquely.

I heaved a deep sigh, but I took the shipping agent's name—he was French. I entered the consulate next door and cooled my heels there for a while until they dug up somebody to take my passport photo. I had a beard, and could think of nothing to smile about, so I hoped I would be recognizable. I then walked straight to the Frenchman's house. As a middleman helping to supply the Americans with international goods in the war effort, he had become very prosperous. He owned a spacious town house with a fancy entrance right on the Saigon River, and servants, including a courtly Vietnamese assistant named Mr. Minh, who spoke French with his boss. He was a thin, elderly gentleman with a dignified bearing who'd be retired if he lived in the States.

The French agent kept me outside as he read my US consulate paper, scowling at it over his reading glasses.

"Wait here!" he barked at me, and I peeked in as he shuffled through the chandeliered foyer into a book-lined room. He brought back about $40 in cash. The union required that while a seaman was on the beach in a foreign port, the shipping company had to pay him daily until everything got sorted out. That would be enough for three hots and a cot every day if I was careful. All I had to do was come to the Frenchman's house each day to pick up my pay. This is one of the reasons I have been a union man all my life. It was union struggles that won benefits for seamen stuck on land. They don't simply hand that stuff to working people without a fight, and I had the first fighting seafarer, Joseph Curran, who was charged with mutiny for his efforts, to thank for it. God bless the National Maritime Union. It provided a smidge of good news in what was becoming a pretty bleak situation.

CHAPTER 16

AMERICAN MONEY IS GOOD FOR BRIBES

I soon found out how expensive everything was in Saigon. So, I asked around, and I learned of a Korean hotel that cost about a quarter the price of the ones in which Americans usually stayed in the capital. It would leave me enough money each day for a couple of decent meals and a beer. It was in Cholon, which was essentially Saigon's Chinatown, with about a half million residents of Chinese descent. I regretted that the government had closed Cholon's Grand Monde, the biggest casino in Southeast Asia, supposedly because it was being run by river pirates. Maybe the officials weren't getting a big enough cut. But tucked away in the alleyways were small gambling joints, like Lo Tien (Happy Skies) and Hai Tien (Sea Skies). Word was you could find American generals playing blackjack in there.

I went into the hotel and said to the old man at the desk, "How are you, sir?" in the basic Japanese I had learned in the marines. Most older Koreans speak Japanese because in 1910 their country had been unwillingly annexed by Japan and their own language forbidden.

He answered, *Genkidesu, arigatō*—"I am doing well, thank you." His low rates were good enough for me. I wasn't looking for tennis courts and spa treatments. I checked in. And, keeping a promise to the Beechcraft pilot, the first thing I did was to take a long shower. I still didn't have a change of clothes, but I washed out my shirt and underwear, wrung them out, and then let them dry out in the Saigon sun. Every day, I went back to the French agent's house for my cash, then on to the US consulate to see my buddy Heller, checking in to see if they had received my passport. This went on for about four days. Meanwhile, my ship was sailing farther and farther away. I kept trying to convince Heller to skip the formalities:

"I've gone around the world three times without a passport," I implored him. "I spent five months in the US Marine Corps in Subic Bay in the Philippines; I know my way around there. Why can't you put me on a military transport plane to Clark Air Base on Luzon Island, and I can fly to Manila from there? You must have planes going there all day long bringing boys out and bringing boys in."

Heller didn't feel like getting creative with my case. But, finally, the passport came in. There it was, its blank pages somehow full of promise, stamped January 26, 1968—exactly a week after my arrival—and bearing a photo of me looking rather grim.

I was happy now, but just for a minute, because Heller reminded me that this was only half of it. Now I had to bring the passport to the State Department of South Vietnam and obtain an exit visa. And it wouldn't be cheap. Heller said I would have to bribe the clerk there about 9,000 *piastres*—roughly $900.

I said to him, "You know I'm living on forty dollars a day! Where the hell do you think I'm going to find nine hundred bucks?'

"Don't worry," Heller replied. "We'll *lend* you the money." He was obviously used to this. I signed for the "loan."

With that, Heller took a grey lockbox out of his drawer, counted out some cash, and slid the money in an envelope and sealed it. He called over one of the younger consular officials and, handing him the envelope, told him to escort me to the South Vietnamese State Department Building.

We went over there, and the lines wrapped out the door and around the building. It was like the movie *Casablanca*: people waiting, waiting, waiting to leave the Vichy-controlled Moroccan city as they fled the Nazis, and some never would. I had it a bit easier because the consular official was with me; still, it took about two hours of going from window to window, filling out paperwork. Then we sat down with the guy who was going to receive the "fee."

The young guy oversaw the whole transaction, I didn't so much as touch the money. I don't think that he or Heller got kickbacks—he just didn't trust me with the $900. But here was my country condoning the official corruption rampant in the South Vietnamese government during the war. I appreciated the American taxpayers back in the States who would pay $900 to Uncle Sam that year to cover my bribe.

I showed him my shiny new passport—which, after all that trouble, didn't interest him in the slightest—and then I handed over the fat envelope of cash. How do you like this:

the arrogant fellow had the nerve to count it. In front of the US consulate official! He made some kind of checkmark on one of my forms and then said, "We will notify the American consulate when your visa is ready." He wouldn't even give it to me then and there. Hurry up and wait. My ship would surely be out in the Pacific Ocean halfway to the States by the time the visa came through.

CHAPTER 17

THE CARAVELLE
ROOFTOP BAR

I had to find a job. I was essentially living in Saigon now, and I knew how to live on the cheap, but I didn't know how long this was going to be, and $40 a day wasn't cracking it. They said there were no jobs at the embassy. But I know how to mix drinks; I went from bar to bar asking the Vietnamese managers for bartender positions. For some reason, they thought that was hilarious. To a man, they laughed, some uproariously, and I couldn't convince them.

Meanwhile, I was still here, and there was the matter of the other guys on my list, such as Richard Reynolds, a second lieutenant in the Marine Corps. I couldn't miss Joey McFadden, an electrician who would later, in 1974, be found screaming by relief pitcher Tug McGraw after he'd fractured his leg after falling twenty feet off the scoreboard at Shea Stadium. Bobby Pappas was out there, too, in the huge headquarters and ammo base Long Binh, with fifty thousand other GIs who had just been visited by entertainers Bob Hope, Barbara McNair, and Raquel

Welch at Christmas. I thought it was unfair that Bobby had been drafted in September at the age of twenty-three; he was married with a kid and had worked for the Army Corps of Engineers to boot. Other guys might have tried to wriggle out of it, but Bobby went. I really wanted to bring him that beer and everybody's good wishes. I had to check in with the American consulate every day, though, which meant I had to stay local.

Looking for work around Saigon, I saw how colorful it was. I had been in Japan, and that was exotic and civilized at the same time. But wartime Saigon was colorful in a chaotic, more Third World way. There were bustling outdoor markets full of people selling everything from silk dresses to flattened ducks to exotic birds in cages, all hanging from hooks side by side. The French, despite their unwelcome ten-decade colonization of Vietnam, from Napoleon III's conquering of Da Nang in 1858 until the last French soldier left in 1956, had at least built all sorts of beautiful, white stucco buildings and town houses and churches under a colonnade of giant palm trees. It was like dunking parts of Paris into the tropics.

The French had built the Continental Palace Hotel in 1880 to remind them of Paris. It was a beautiful wedding cake of a place now said to be run by the son of a Corsican gangster. I went in for a drink a couple of times and snuck upstairs to see room 214, where the English novelist Graham Greene wrote *The Quiet American* while covering the French Indochina War in the early 1950s.

But I received glares for my raggedy appearance—I must have looked even worse than the many journalists who hung out in the bar—so I went elsewhere. There were still fancy *colons* living in Saigon who'd go there, as well as any bigs coming to Vietnam, such as executives conducting business with the military. They would have stayed at the Continental Palace.

The Caravelle Hotel was more my cup of tea—or glass of beer, if you will. It was owned by Australians and guarded by Australian marines, because their embassy was inside. The Australians, allies of ours, had about 7,500 troops there at the time and 60,000 over the course of the war. Some 3,500 New Zealanders also served.

So that's where the Aussies, New Zealanders, Canadians, the Irish, the Brits, and other American cousins—people able to have a good time even in the middle of hell—would congregate. They appreciated the view from the Caravelle's glorious rooftop bar as much as I did. So did many of the journalists from all over the world covering the war. CBS foreign correspondent Morley Safer was living and working at the Caravelle in 1965, when his report on US Marines being ordered to burn down the hamlet of Cam Ne aired on the *CBS Evening News with Walter Cronkite*. A livid President Johnson reportedly called network president Frank Stanton and said, "Your boys shat on the American flag yesterday," and he ordered that Safer be investigated for Communist ties. When LBJ was told that Safer wasn't Communist, he was Canadian, the president reportedly said, "Well, I knew there was *something* wrong with him."

Most of the hotels had moved their bars to the rooftops following so many bar bombings early in the war—but the Caravelle bar was the best. With so many reporters and displaced persons favoring the joint, the beer and stories flowed for a mighty *craic*, so that's where I went for the duration.

Finally, one day at my daily check-in at the consulate, the clerk ran his finger down a list on a page and said, "Donohue, John? Yes, your visa was approved."

"Thank God."

"That's the good news."

"What?! What's the bad news?" I asked.

"Well, your ship has left Manila."

"Now, *that's* a surprise!" I yelled sarcastically. "I should have placed a bet on it!"

However, the official continued, another ship in Manila would be loading cargo for a few days, and its captain had agreed to take me on. He said there was an early flight out of Tan Son Nhut Air Base the next day, Wednesday, January 31, 1968.

"Don't party too hardy tonight," he advised. "Traffic might be bad leaving the city tomorrow. It's their New Year's, you know."

Oh, I knew it: the Caravelle staff had been hinting about tips all week. It was the Lunar New Year, which lasts for days. They told me it was called Tet, and that it's a bigger deal than ours. The Vietnamese travel back to their home villages and visit family and honor their ancestors. The reporters hanging out at the Caravelle had told us that Ho Chi Minh and General Giap had sought a Tet holiday truce and that President Johnson had agreed to it. According to the journos, "LBJ's even going to stop bombing the North."

I thanked the clerk and hustled over to the South Vietnamese State Department.

"Donohue?"

"Yeah?"

"Happy New Year, man."

CHAPTER 18

FINDING A SEAFARING FRIEND

I had my passport, I had my visa; I was feeling as if I had my act together for the first time in a while. It was a good feeling, so I headed over to Tu Do Street to celebrate with a beer. I saw a bar I hadn't been to before and looked through the window to check it out; I did a double take. Inside, sitting on a bar stool like it was old home week, was Johnny Jackson (not his real name), a merchant mariner from New Jersey with whom I'd sailed before. I always loved hanging out with him because he knew the great places in all the ports. He was older than I was and had seen it all.

I went in and slapped him on the back.

"Let me see your ID, sailor!" I shouted.

Johnny actually started to reach into his pocket, and then he looked up at me, and his eyes bugged.

"Chickie!?!" He laughed and shook his head.

"Johnny! How are ya, man?"

"What ship are you on, Chick?"

My long-awaited passport, issued by the US embassy in Saigon after a bureaucratic nightmare worthy of Catch-22. I look a little worse for wear, I'd say.

"I'm on the beach," I said.

"You're on the beach in Saigon?!"

"Well, it's a long story to tell, and I'm a bit thirsty."

We sat there for a couple of hours, trading tales. Johnny was on the SS *Limon*, delivering a huge cargo of frozen food to the military, everything from steaks to blueberries.

"Hey, Johnny," I said. "Why don't we pay the *Limon* a visit?"

The white-hulled refrigerator ship, built in 1945 as World War II neared its end, loomed above the sampans in the Saigon River like a giant Frigidaire, capable of chilling seven thousand tons of perishables on the long, slow journey across the Pacific. The *Limon*, part of the United Fruit Company's Great White Fleet used during peacetime to bring bananas and other produce to the United States from Central America, was now sailing for the US Navy as part of the Military Sea Transportation Service.

Vietnamese port security personnel let me onto the pier, and the MPs on the boat let me board the *Limon* with Johnny after I showed my seaman's documents. Johnny brought me right down to the freezer and opened it wide.

It had everything: lobster, hamburgers, strawberry ice cream, you name it. Any food that could be frozen, they had it. I don't know who it was all headed for—not just officers, I hoped. Johnny invited me to join the other seamen for dinner, which was prepared from the delicacies they were delivering. Johnny told them my situation, and when it was time to go, they gave me some fresh clothes and $100 they had quietly collected. They were in my union and they treated me like a brother. I'll never forget it. The beer and lobster would have been enough.

Johnny took me aside and said, "Listen, man, look up."

"What?" I said. "The Southern Cross?"—the constellation that sailors long ago took as a blessing on their voyage.

"No, the moon, man! Up there!" he said, pointing.

"It's only a pale sliver," I said.

"Exactly. And tomorrow, it'll be gone. You know what that means now in 'Nam?"

"No, I don't."

"It's New Year's Eve! It's like in Chinatown back home: they base it on the first new moon—no moon—when the night is darkest. They honor their great-great-great-grandparents and make wishes for the coming year. They call it Tet. They've called a truce! It's party time, man!

"Listen," he went on, "I've got a girlfriend here who I see each time I'm in port. She runs a little dance hall south of here. I'm gonna go see her tonight; why don't you come along? The place is a blast. I can ask one of the guys to lend you some nice clothes." I didn't want to blow my flight in the morning. But I felt buoyed by the feed we'd had and the extra cash. I felt I could handle it all, so I said, "Why not? I'll be able to make some Vietnamese New Year's resolutions."

CHAPTER 19

HAPPY NEW YEAR, BABY

Two guys taking fares on their motor scooters drove us to the nightspot, about a half hour down the Saigon River. It was a little place, half wood, half bamboo, up on stilts over the water. Christmas lights were strung around the edge of the thatched roof and, incredibly, the sound of the Shirelles singing "Soldier Boy" echoed out of the place. Johnny's lady friend jumped with joy at the sight of him and gave him a big hug. I was surprised to hear my friend from Bayonne exchange sweet nothings with her in French, and then she asked, in English, "You bring me some American records, Johnny?"

"Of course, I did, baby—the latest!" He handed her a stack of 45s. Then he started squeezing her and saying stuff in French that made her giggle.

She didn't have a jukebox, but she did have a little turquoise turntable, and she squealed as she popped on the stack, and down dropped Sam and Dave's "Soul Man." She and Johnny, and most every woman in the place, started shimmying. I went to the bar, where there were only two or three guys, and ordered a beer.

I watched the ladies dance with each other in their colorful silk *ao dais*. Those were the tight tunics with a long slit up the side that all the young women wore over silken pants. I had asked Mr. Minh, my buddy at the French shipping agent's house, about it. Back home, girls and young women were still getting suspended if they tried to wear pants to school, and such garb was strictly forbidden for any women in the military and frowned upon in the office. But in Vietnam, all women wore this dress-pants combo.

Mr. Minh explained: "One day in the seventeen hundreds, one of the Nguyen dynasty lords—they controlled the South— decreed that every man *and* woman in his court *must* wear a silk gown over pants. The *ao dai*. Lord Nguyen—he was by all accounts a very macho dude, with sixteen sons—wanted to distinguish his court from that of his enemies, the Trinh lords who controlled the North out of Hanoi. Even back then, our slender nation was divided. Up there, both male and female aristocrats wore tunics over skirts. He wanted to be different. But it was also about status.

"We learned in school that King Louis XIV of France declared that both men and women in his court at Versailles should wear red high heels. This was one of the things they did to show off the fact that they didn't have to work, because French peasants weren't about to wear such shoes working in the fields. It was the same with the *ao dai,* because you need a lot of silk to make one. Back then, only the aristocrats could afford silk, and they wore layers and layers of it to show off, no matter how hot it was. They'd rather have sweated like pigs than look poor."

He laughed, then added: "But even though women are covered from neck to ankle to wrist with this traditional outfit, if you don't mind my saying so, I still think it's very sensual. We have a saying: 'The *ao dai* covers everything but hides nothing.'"

As the girls danced together to "Soul Man," I could see what he meant. They looked to be in their late teens, early twenties. They had their hair teased up in bouffants like the Supremes, and a few were real beauties, except maybe a little sad around the eyes. I wondered if they had boyfriends who were off fighting and if their fathers and brothers were gone, too. I knew they were in this joint for the money, but they were young enough that they seemed to actually be trying to have a bit of fun in the middle of the war.

The bright brass section opening of Aretha Franklin's "Respect" blasted out, and a young woman in a blue *ao dai* came up. She had a limp.

"You buy me Saigon tea, sir?"

"Sure, why not? Barkeep, a Saigon tea for the lady, please."

Saigon teas are alcohol-free but she tossed it back like it was a shot of whiskey—maybe for New Year's, they were being beneficent and spiking them. She yelled, *"Danse avec moi!"* over the music, grabbing my hands. Seeing my quizzical grin, she tilted her head and looked at me with one eye closed. "Hmmm . . . red, long hair. Not soldier. Australian?"

"I do not have that honor."

"Irish?"

"Well, those are the ancestors I worship. I'm American, but no longer a soldier."

"Okay, Red! Dance with me!"

I took her hand, and we walked to the dance floor, where I did my trademark stay-in-one-spot, side-to-side double bop. She was smiling, following along, when the next record dropped, and the menacing voice of the Doors' Jim Morrison intoned, "*You know that it would be untrue, you know that I would be a liar . . .*"

It really wasn't a song you could double bop to. I pulled Lady in Blue closer to me, and we kind of rocked each other in a slow dance.

"What's your name?" I asked.

"Dao," she said. "It means 'peach blossom.' "

"I don't think I've ever seen one."

"I have one here," she said, opening the slit of her *ao dai*. A long scar ran up the inside of her thigh. Over it, she'd gotten a tattoo of a branch intertwined with delicate pink flowers.

"Beautiful," I said. I didn't ask her how she'd gotten the scar. I wondered if it was a shrapnel wound caused by us or the Commies.

"Yes, it's considered one of the most beautiful flowers, especially now at Tet time," she explained. "We lay peach blossoms on the altar to our ancestors, along with five of the most delicious fruits, so that our loved ones who are gone might have the most wonderful things again . . ."

She paused for a minute, and then said, wistfully, "We used to have many wonderful things here."

I looked deep into her brown eyes. Those eyes reminded me of the line from a poem I read in high school, by the French surrealist writer André Breton, and never forgot: She had *"eyes like wood always under the axe / eyes of water to be drunk in prison."* It was understandable. I had been singing "Auld Lang Syne" myself a few weeks before.

"Tet—that's your New Year's, isn't it?" I asked.

"Yes," she said absently.

"What year is it?"

"It's going to be 4847—almost 5000! We are very old!"

"Wow. Our calendar is half that, and America is even younger. We drink champagne on our New Year's and sing a song to remind us of old friends and acquaintances," I said.

"We remember our grandparents, and we give the children new clothes and a little money in red envelopes. Red is the color of New Year's because the beast Nian, who eats children, is afraid of it and won't come near if he sees it. So, you bring me protection from the beast, Red!"

"I guess that's kind of like our bogeyman, but he's year-round. We make resolutions; do you?"

"Revolutions?!" She gave me a sidelong glance.

"No, ha ... *resolutions*. They are promises to yourself to be better. To make good changes in the new year. But we forget about them by Saint Patrick's Day."

"Is that when you have those big fireworks shows?"

"No, we have a big parade that day. We have our big fireworks on the Fourth of July. That's our Independence Day; the day we won our freedom from the British."

"Like the French have Bastille Day."

"Yes, except the French gained their freedom by ending their own monarchy. We won our democracy by ousting our colonial rulers, the British."

"Hmmmm ..." There was an awkward pause.

"Tell me something, Red," she ventured. "How come the French and you Americans are so proud of your revolutions and your independence, but you won't let other people have theirs? Do you know we have been fighting for our independence since Jesus walked the Earth?"

I started to wonder if she was a VC Mata Hari—the exotic dancer who spied for the Germans in World War I. Luckily, I didn't have any state secrets for her to get out of me.

"Well," I replied. "I wouldn't call marching in step with Mao and Moscow 'independence.'"

"They want to bully us, too. Everybody wants to dominate us, a tiny little country. And you and they are so big and have so much! Sometimes I wonder if we have gold or rubies or diamonds hidden in our hills that we don't know about, but you do. I don't get it, as the GIs say."

I had to admit, she was gutsy. Or emboldened by spiked Saigon tea, who knows? I thought about launching into the domino theory, that if Vietnam fell into Communist hands, then Laos would go, and then Cambodia, and then Thailand. Then Malaysia, Burma, Indonesia, and maybe even Australia would be threatened, and India. But I didn't feel like it.

"Hey, it's New Year's Eve, beautiful. Do you really want to talk politics? Tell me what you wish for tonight."

"We wish for health and wealth and luck . . . "

"I could use some of that right now: luck."

"And, if you are not married, we wish you, '*Chuc mau chong tim duoc nguoi yeu,*'" she said, and started giggling like crazy.

"Wow, that must be good. What is it?"

"I don't want to tell you," she said, giggling some more.

"Aw, come on. I'll buy you another Saigon tea."

"Okay! It means, 'May you find new love in the new year,'" she said, still giggling.

She took my hand and brought me to the bamboo railing overlooking the river. The fingernail moon cut into the black waters, the road now a charcoal smudge. A thousand cherry bombs convulsed the night.

"Tet—it's almost here," she said.

"Well, in that case," I said, "let's celebrate."

In the wee hours, Johnny came out of the room where he had been with his lady friend and said he had to return to the ship. I had to catch that flight to Manila in the morning—only a few hours from now. I probably shouldn't have been out carousing. The bartender and another guy were hanging around, waiting for us to leave.

"They're missing their holiday," I said. "I feel bad."

"Don't," said Johnny. "They've been happy to see us, because unlike GIs, they know seamen were paid in American dollars. Dollars are worth five to ten times more on the black market here. That's why Charlie rarely attacks seamen."

Johnny asked the guys if they could give us rides back to Saigon, and they were glad for the gig. We said our good-byes. I didn't want to give Dao some bullcrap that I'd see her again. I might have if I were staying in country, but I was blowing this pop stand.

I told her, "I wish you health and wealth. And, as the Irish say: 'For every storm, a rainbow; for every tear, a smile; for every sigh, a sweet song; and an answer for each prayer.'"

Dao looked like she was used to good-byes.

"*Chuc mau chong tim duoc nguoi yeu,*" she said, and she gave me a sad little smile.

"You, too," I said.

Johnny and I descended the rickety steps, and we hopped on the backs of the bartenders' motorcycles and took off.

We had asked them to stop at a fork in the road. Johnny headed toward the docks, and I was headed back to Cholon. Chinatown.

Johnny had helped put me back together better than Humpty Dumpty, and now I was shipshape to leave Vietnam. I kind of awkwardly leaned over and gave him a one-armed hug.

"See ya back home," I said.

"You got it, buddy," Johnny replied.

We roared off in our different directions. I took another look in the sky. The thin crescent moon was gone.

CHAPTER 20

BEAUCOUP VC

The fireworks were getting incredibly loud as we got closer to Saigon. South Vietnam's president, Nguyen van Thieu, had lifted a ban on fireworks that had been in effect for years, and I had seen all manner of them being sold in the markets. People had strung them in long red chains from their eaves in anticipation of the day. What a cacophony they produced. I wondered if kids were putting M-80 firecrackers in garbage cans for a bigger bang, like we used to do in New York.

Back at the hotel, in the lobby, the manager had strung little red and gold envelopes around the desk, probably in hope of tips. I rang the bell, and he came out of the back room, rubbing his eyes. I felt bad about waking him up, but I wanted to pay the bill and remind him that he was driving me to the American embassy before dawn to connect with the military transport to Tan Son Nhut Air Base in the morning. He'd remembered. I asked him to wake me up at five in the morning—in just two hours. I hoped he wouldn't sleep through it. The flight wasn't until eleven, but I wasn't taking any chances.

I saw that his dusty altar to Buddha up in the corner was now sparkly and festooned with fruits and flowers. *"Dao?"* I asked, pointing to the buds. *"Dao,"* he answered, nodding and looking surprised.

I went up to my room and quickly threw my stuff into a bag. I didn't have much. Then I collapsed on the bed, but I needn't have worried about not waking up in time. The *boom-boom-boom* was ridiculously loud, and I tried to fall asleep through it for an hour, to no avail.

Man, these people really love their New Year's fireworks, I thought.

At that moment, something burst through my window. Glass shattered all over the floor, and I heard yelling in the street.

What the hell?! I thought. *Traffic is gonna be murder in this New Year's chaos—I gotta vamoose.* I grabbed my bag and tore down the stairs. It was a little after four o'clock.

The lobby was empty. I yelled over the front desk into the back room:

"Papasan! Papasan! Doko iku no?!! Where are you? I need a ride to the American embassy *now!* I'll pay you double!"

The manager came running out and seemed to crouch behind the desk. He started screaming at me in Korean. Somehow I thought he was screaming at me to keep quiet, which was ironic. Then he switched to French.

"Beaucoup VC!" he yelled.

Beaucoup VC? You know, *beaucoup*—that's French for *"a lot,"* or, as we used to say in New York when we won big in a card game or bet, "boocoo" bucks. I hadn't seen *anybody* on the ride home, let alone VC. What was he talking about? The dozen or so guys I had heard yelling a few minutes before? I kept pressing him to leave; I offered him almost every American dollar I had left.

He was frantic. He looked like he would do anything to be rid of me. He shouted at me in Japanese to follow him. It was pitch black out—no moon. We ran out the back to his car, jumped in, and sped off at about ninety miles per hour. I mean, I was in a hurry to reach the embassy, but this was ridiculous. He was in a panic. But he was racing down all the side streets instead of the main drag, and I thought, *We'll never get there at this rate. Why the hell is he taking this route?* I looked up and down, and absolutely nobody was on the streets. Sleeping off the celebratory drinking of the night before, I figured. There wasn't a vehicle or a person moving; not even a cat. But there were choppers overhead. Then the car squealed to a stop.

Concertina wire was strung across the street on all four corners, blocking the entire intersection. Something was wrong, but not wrong enough that I wouldn't keep heading to the embassy.

Papasan drove up on the sidewalk and down about a block when suddenly cops surrounded us. These were the South Vietnamese National Police—called White Mice by the people both for their white shirts and for the lack of respect they were given. There were about ten of them, pointing their machine guns into the car and screaming at us in Vietnamese.

I was yelling back, "Okay! Okay! Calm down! Take it easy!" I didn't want either of us killed by South Vietnamese "friendly fire."

I had about fifty bucks in my pocket. I gave *Papasan* forty-eight of it and said in his native Korean (that, out of respect, I had finally been learning), "*Annyeong, Abeonim, gam sa ham ni da*." Good-bye, Pops; thanks for everything. I've got a plane to catch.

I didn't know what the hell was going on, but I was still of the mind-set that if I made it to the embassy, my ride would be awaiting me. We would glide off to the airport, and I would be on my merry way to catch up with my ship in Manila and then back home.

Man, was I in denial.

I gingerly stepped out of the car and said, "American embassy," over and over. Maybe they thought I worked there. They let me walk away. They couldn't have cared less about me.

I continued along the Saigon River until I got to the Hotel Majestic, a beautiful, old French colonial hotel. From its rooftop, you could see the village on the other side of the river, which still had farm patches and thatch-roofed huts. It had always reminded me of New York, where you have New Jersey's tree-covered Palisades cliffs on the west bank of the Hudson, right across from our metropolis.

But now it was anything but peaceful. Armed men, not in uniform, were outside the Majestic speaking English—they were Americans.

"What the hell's going on?" I asked.

"Beaucoup VC, man," one said.

Now even the Americans are saying it, I thought.

"Whaddaya mean?" I pressed.

"The Vietcong attacked Saigon a couple of hours ago," another guy said. "They got half of Cholon. There's fighting all over Saigon; they're trying to take the whole city."

"What?! Well, I gotta get to the American embassy," I

insisted irrationally. It sure as hell hadn't been cherry bombs I'd heard exploding all night.

"*Charlie has the embassy, man!*" he yelled. "The MPs and marines are in there fighting them off!"

Vietcong guerrillas had overrun the United States embassy? How could that be possible?

Three personnel carriers screeched up, and about ten American commandos, armed like Rambo, jumped out. They had every freaking gun going. They looked up and down the street and then escorted some VIP, whose face I couldn't see, into the Majestic. It could have been Ambassador Ellsworth Bunker, for all I know. But the guys looked beat to hell—they had been through more than one firefight to bring him here.

I could hear gunfire coming from the South Vietnamese navy headquarters across the street and from somewhere across the river. I headed up Tu Do Street, and it looked like the streets in that 1959 sci-fi movie starring Harry Belafonte, *The World, the Flesh and the Devil*, about the end of the world. Nobody. Zip. Not a sign of life, except maybe the furtive movement of a curtain up above. I thought that if I could maneuver down the five blocks to the embassy, I would be safe. I still didn't believe that Charlie had really taken it. Maybe there was still armed transport running to the Tan Son Nhut military airfield. But I had no idea who was hiding in what doorway, so I inched along close to the buildings and the stucco walls in between.

I was almost at the Brinks Hotel, which during wartime had been transformed into the US Army Bachelors Officers' Quarters. It had been kind of a swinging place until the Vietcong blew it up on Christmas Eve 1964, killing two officers and wounding sixty people celebrating the holiday. Security had been beefed up ever since, but now the Brinks resembled a fortress. There was an armored vehicle outside, MPs armed to the teeth all around the perimeter, and sandbags piled up at the front.

"Did the VC get in here?!" I asked an MP.

"No, but they've got our embassy, they've got the airfield at Tan Son Nhut, and they're trying to take the Presidential Palace right now. VC and the NVA have hit every town in the country, man!"

They got the airfield, too?! General Westmoreland had his huge Military Assistance Command, Vietnam (MACV) headquarters, known as Pentagon East, at Tan Son Nhut. How could that be possible? I pictured a few VC invading the airfield and being quickly dispatched by our MPs. Little did I know that three entire battalions of Vietcong had invaded the airfield, with only one small force of the 716th Military Police and two companies of the South Vietnamese army fighting them off, sustaining heavy casualties, until tanks from the 25th Infantry Division arrived.

"You'll have to move along, sir," the MP said.

I wanted to move along, but I didn't like this guy telling me to.

"Lemme get this straight," I said. "You're telling me that the VC have invaded Saigon, and this is a US Army outpost, and I'm an American, and you're telling me to move along? Where the hell do you want me to go?"

I thought my army existed to protect American civilians first and foremost.

"I'm sorry, but you can't stay here, sir. I've got my orders."

"I've heard that before," I said.

CHAPTER 21

BROKEN TRUCE

I would find out later that several thousand guerrilla fighters had attacked Saigon, part of a force of eighty-four thousand North Vietnamese army and Vietcong soldiers who'd invaded a hundred towns and key military sites all over South Vietnam, in what came to be known as the Tet offensive. It had been masterminded by General Giap and his military logistician, Le Duan, who took advantage of LBJ's acceptance of a New Year's truce to launch the attack. It was the definition of perfidy.

A month before, the United States had entrusted the security of Saigon to the South Vietnamese National Police, after our military and police had provided extensive training. General Giap must have realized the vulnerability there. He believed that if his army and the Vietcong could overtake strategic sites such as the US embassy, the Presidential Palace, the airfield, and the radio station, then the people of Saigon and the other cities under attack would join them in an uprising. At the very least, it would look extremely bad to Americans back home watching it on the evening news.

For three months, the enemy had been bringing into the towns weapons and ammunition hidden in vegetable trucks. Now, soldiers themselves had infiltrated under the guise of travelers headed home to ancestral villages for the Lunar New Year, for which a five-day truce had been declared.

They broke the truce and attacked Saigon and major US bases and airfields at Chu Lai, Phu Bai, and Tan Son Nhut, as well as key American installations at An Khe and Vinh Long. The US military leadership had received intelligence that something big was about to happen, but it underestimated how big. The death toll in the two-month period of Tet, from January 29 through March 31, 1968, was 3,895 American servicemen, 14,300 civilians, 4,954 South Vietnamese soldiers, 214 allies, and 58,373 North Vietnamese and Vietcong forces.

Many Americans wondered how tens of thousands of troops could "sneak" into South Vietnam armed with artillery, weapons, and ammo, and catch our military leaders so unprepared. The map tells part of the story. Vietnam, shaped like a dog bone, is so narrow in its middle that it's only thirty miles wide in places. Laos and Cambodia form another dog bone next to it. North Vietnamese troops would hike south through the jungle along the Ho Chi Minh Trail, down through Laos and then Cambodia, to infiltrate South Vietnam from the west.

Another factor was that our political and military leaders thought the North Vietnamese would never violate the deeply religious holiday. Westmoreland called it "Christmas, Thanksgiving, and the Fourth of July rolled into one."

Eight NVA battalions overtook Hue, the old imperial city, and the marines and the army had to fight them off for twenty-five days. Two battalions invaded Ban Me Thuot; two battalions attacked Qui Nhon, where Tommy Collins was; and two attacked Nha Trang. Three battalions attacked the city of Kon Tum, and three more battalions took over Tan Son Nhut Air Base outside Saigon, home to General Westmoreland's headquarters. The 716th and 92nd Military Police Battalions at Tan Son Nhut fought them off in a seven-hour gunfight. While most places were retaken within days, even hours, fighting in Hue, Da Lat, Pleiku, and other sites would go on for weeks. Seven US Army battalions moved into Saigon.

General Giap's uprising never materialized, but he won the propaganda war on day one: when the American people saw that our embassy and Westmoreland's own military headquarters had been under siege, mistrust of White House and military claims and antiwar sentiment grew.

I didn't take this picture, but it captures a moment I was terribly familiar with: two soldiers hide behind a tree in front of the US embassy on Thong Nhut Boulevard as the embassy was taken over by Vietcong guerrillas on the first night of the Tet offensive. I did the exact same thing and count myself lucky to have survived that harrowing evening.

CHAPTER 22

THE AMERICAN EMBASSY
UNDER SIEGE

Banished from Brinks, I continued to inch along the wall on Thong Nhut Boulevard toward the embassy. I wanted to be nearby when we took it back, which I thought would be instantly. I didn't know yet how few of our soldiers were inside the compound, nor how those few had been hamstrung at every turn.

I could see the six-story embassy chancellery building down the wide boulevard lined with consulates. The chancellery, which looked like a giant concrete cheese grater surrounded by an eight-foot-high reinforced concrete wall, had opened in September.

I was only two blocks away now, and the gunfire was growing louder and louder. Chopper blades pummeled the air overhead. There were armed Americans, not in uniform, on the other side of the street, and they hand signaled me to stay on my side.

Just before three in the morning, Vietcong commandos in a taxi had pulled up to the embassy compound side gate and fired AK-47 automatics at the two young MPs guarding it. Specialist Fourth Class (SP4) Charles L. Daniel, of Durham, North Carolina, and Corporal William Sebast, of Albany, New York, fired back as they slammed the gate shut.

"They're coming in! They're coming in!" Daniel radioed. "Help us!"

Some people that day, including me, believed they had opened the gate to let in a longtime embassy driver, who had ID, and whom they never imagined was an undercover VC.

The military told reporters that guerrillas from the highly trained Vietcong C-10 Sapper Battalion jumped out of a truck and within moments blew a three-foot hole in the wall near the side gate. Their leader, Nguyen Van Sau, slipped through first. He was killed immediately by Sebast and Daniel, and so was his second-in-command, who followed behind him, top brass claimed.

Seventeen more VC soldiers, all armed with machine guns, stormed the embassy grounds. Sebast, twenty, and Daniel, twenty-three, fought them off as best they could out in the open until, tragically, they were gunned down.

US Marine Sergeant Ronald W. Harper, twenty, of Cambridge, Minnesota, was on the perimeter when the gunfire erupted. Aware that personnel were working upstairs in the embassy, he tore across the grounds and into the embassy lobby, past fellow marine George Zahuranic, also twenty, who was putting out a call for help over the radio. Harper bolted shut the huge wooden front doors of the embassy.

Seconds later, an antitank rocket blasted through the embassy wall and exploded in the lobby. Zahuranic, of Uniontown, Pennsylvania, was seriously wounded in the head and chest, and their radio was destroyed. Two more rockets smashed through the lobby. Harper ran to Zahuranic to administer first aid. A sapper threw a grenade through a window grill, and it blew a hole in the marble floor next to them.

Two young MPs, responding to the first radio call for help, sped to the front gate. Sergeant Jonnie B. Thomas, twenty-four, of Detroit and SP4 Owen Mebust, twenty, of Lynwood, California, were ambushed and killed in a fusillade of Russian-made Kalashnikov fire.

The VC cut the phone lines, leaving Harper to guard the embassy's ground floor alone, without communications, and armed with only a .38 pistol, a 12-gauge shotgun, a Beretta M12 submachine gun with pistol cartridges and whatever other ammo he had. He could hear the voices of the VC right outside and had no idea how many of them were out there. Upstairs were three CIA staffers and five others, armed only with pistols. Harper thought he was going to die there, but he was determined not to leave his post or to let the VC inside.

Here's what I mean by hamstrung: although five North Vietnamese army companies had prematurely invaded thirteen cities the night before because they'd used an old calendar to determine New Year's Day, top US brass had taken that clue and put the military on alert, but added exactly *one* extra marine to guard the US embassy building in Saigon, for a total of three marines. They posted Sergeant Rudy Soto of Selma, California, on the roof, armed with a pistol and an M16 rifle, which jammed within minutes of the invasion. As for the consulate building that I had visited so often, top brass deemed it sufficient to have the usual single marine guard it.

At least Soto had a radio on the chancellery rooftop, but because he wasn't getting a response from inside, he assumed that Harper and Zahuranic must be dead. The twenty-five-year-old sergeant did his best with his pistol from six stories up after the seventeen VC commandos took over the grounds.

Meanwhile, Major Hillel Schwartz and other pilots of the 101st Airborne kept trying to land their choppers on the rooftop helipad, but they were driven off repeatedly by a barrage of machine-gun fire. At some point in the night, the wounded Zahuranic was brought to the roof and Schwartz landed only long enough to airlift him out. The major flew back, and he and other chopper pilots with the 101st were hovering above as I moved along the boulevard.

I was going from tree to tree at this point. Some of the palms were three feet wide—the French had planted a canopy along the boulevard, like a tropical Champs-Élysées. Thank God for this vestige of French colonialism. I would hide behind one, dash forward, and then take cover behind the next.

I tried some of the gates and doors of the US Information Agency on my side of the street—they were all locked tight.

I saw no other people, no bikes, scooters—nothing moving—down the side streets. The people had fled their homes in chaos or were in hiding. Saigon cops had quickly blocked the major cross streets with concertina wire. But police in the precinct closest to the embassy and tasked with guarding Thong Nhut Boulevard refused to join American MPs who had sped there in a personnel carrier to pick them up. They reportedly locked up the precinct house and hid.

I started running to the next corner, the last block before the embassy grounds.

In the middle of the side street to my right was a sight that nearly stopped me in my tracks. There was a beautiful old Renault limo, but unfortunately, there was a dead guy in the backseat. And the fellow who probably had been his chauffeur was facedown in the road, a puddle of blood forming a halo around his head.

I reached the corner and hid behind the first tree. As the light was coming up, American MPs and men in civilian dress were shooting rifles into the consulate grounds from my side of the street and the choppers continued to hover. Amid the pitch darkness and hampered communications, our soldiers had no idea how many commandos had invaded the grounds, or whether they were inside the embassy or the consulate buildings, or whether Americans were out on the grounds fighting. They didn't want to shoot an American by mistake.

I read later in the *New York Times* and other papers that US Marine Master Sergeant James Conrad Marshall, a twenty-year-old from Monroeville, Alabama, had been guarding the separate one-story consulate building alone. He courageously fought the invaders from its rooftop until he was shot through the throat by a VC sniper. Marshall was the first marine in history to die defending an American embassy.

At first light, an army MP captain and Paul Healey, a heroic and street-smart twenty-year-old private from Boston, led other MPs in the rescue assault. Healey was literally serving his last day in Vietnam, and others in that situation might have held back, but not this kid. He tried to ram the front gate open with his jeep; when that failed, he ran in front of the gate under VC fire and shot the lock six times before it finally broke off. He jumped on top of the jeep and was shooting at the enemy over the wall. Then the MPs jumped inside.

Armed with an M16, a .45, and a .38, Healey fought off the VC commandos shooting from behind trees. At one point, a nearby commando threw a Chinese grenade at Healey; it landed against his leg. Healey dove behind the guy who threw it, and the grenade killed the VC commando and wounded Healey's hand. Down to three bullets, the young private yelled, "The next person who comes in without ammunition, I'm going to shoot *him*."

Another VC sapper came from behind the embassy, and Healey shot him. His Boston street instincts told him there were more where that sapper had come from, and there were: three, whom he fought off.

The MPs knew that the unarmed mission coordinator, retired colonel George Jacobson, and another unarmed staffer had been trapped inside the US mission villa during the entire invasion. Healey ran through a hail of bullets toward the villa, as Colonel Jacobson testified later, and he spotted a pair of bloody sandals outside the door. He and a marine went in shooting side by side; the VC guerrilla shot the marine in the groin, and Healey pulled him back out to safety.

Healey then looked up and saw Colonel Jacobson in a second-floor window. "I realized Jacobson didn't have anything," he told writer Ron Steinman later. "I went out and took my .45, and I threw it up to him. It took about ten throws to get it up to him."

Jacobson caught the gun, turned, and was face-to-face with the guerrilla, who shot at him but missed. Jacobson then killed him with Healey's .45.

I saw one of the army choppers land on the roof of the embassy. After a few minutes, it took off, and then another chopper touched down for a few minutes and left. I couldn't see up there, but I assumed they were landing personnel.

I found out later that seven of our choppers, with paratroopers from the 502nd Infantry's C Company, had finally been able to land on the embassy roof. Inside, they found the staffers armed with pistols in a top-secret communications room.

The ground started to vibrate, and one of our tanks rumbled from the side street to the front of the embassy. I watched as its turret turned, and *boom!* The cannon blasted a hole in the embassy wall. It was a bizarre thing to witness: one of our own tanks shooting at a US diplomatic compound—and, at that point in the battle, unnecessarily. I believe brass at the very top ordered it done so they could claim sappers blew a hole in the wall to cover their own woeful decision to underman security of our embassy when an invasion had already begun up north twenty-four hours before. The US ambassador's driver, once inside, may have simply killed the two MPs and let all his compadres in the gate.

About this time, all gunfire from inside the compound ceased. I heard someone shout, "Hold your fire!"

After a while, I started to see MPs and marine guards and paratroopers and civilians moving around in the courtyard. I wanted to stay out of their way, so I went around to the side street, Mac Dinh Chi Street, to the vehicle entrance.

On the sidewalk, just inside the side gate, the two young MPs lay dead on the ground, with their MP brothers guarding them. I paused and said a prayer.

I saw ten or twelve dead Vietcong in their black clothes and red armbands lying near the planters around the trees. Other dead VC had disguised themselves in South Vietnamese army uniforms.

Somebody who worked at the embassy told me that two of the dead guerrillas had embassy employee IDs on them. The one who had been a driver at the embassy for years had most recently served as Ambassador Ellsworth Bunker's chauffeur. He'd probably gotten an earful of intelligence tooling around Saigon with the ambassador in the back. Some say the plan was to obtain the classified documents and bring them to General Giap—that's probably why the CIA agents were guarding them upstairs.

It took only nineteen VC guerrillas to take over our embassy at three in the morning and hold it until our troops took it back around nine o'clock. Seventeen of the Vietcong were killed, two captured.

I looked at the bodies lying on the ground, and wondered how could they have thought for a second that they would succeed in overtaking and holding the US embassy. And, of course, they didn't. They had to know they were going to be killed. There was no way they could stay there; the next day, the whole place would be exactly as it was before. But they would be dead. It was dumb dedication, I thought. But if, to them, success was getting in there and sounding a wakeup call back in the States, well, they had succeeded. The American public was shocked that our new, fortified embassy and all of Saigon—the capital of South Vietnam—had been overrun by the North Vietnamese and the Vietcong during the Tet offensive. These men in their black pajamas died young for General Giap's propaganda coup. Then he lived to the ripe old age of 102.

People were milling around in the compound, and there was confusion, so I went in. The concrete facade had been shredded in three places by Soviet antitank rockets, and bazooka rockets had pierced holes in the wall around the grounds. Five or six more dead North Vietnamese guerrillas were on the grass and in the driveway. They were thin, but I was surprised at how strong they looked. Most looked to be the same age as our boys.

I went inside, and it wasn't as if staffers had gone back to work, hands folded on their desks, waiting to continue the quotidian business of the embassy and help me on my merry way. No, it was all military now, frantically trying to answer the question *"How the hell did this happen?"*

I saw one guy I knew.

"How many of them were there?! Did any of them get into the embassy?" I asked him.

"There were nineteen of them, and they never got in!" he said. "The paratroopers landed on the roof and went through floor by floor. They found about eight staffers upstairs—one of them was hiding under a bed.

"One lone marine kept firing at them from the lobby all night long," he continued. "He had a partner on the shift who was wounded pretty bad from minute one. Another marine was guarding the consulate alone, and he got killed trying to shoot from the roof. Listen, man, I gotta go—Westmoreland's on his way over here."

It made me proud to have been a marine.

I was wandering around the embassy, and nobody questioned me. I guess they assumed I had a purpose, like I was one of the armed men in plain clothes I had seen fighting outside, who were undoubtedly CIA. But then I found him: the guy I called Heller the Bureaucrat. Now I called him Heller the Hero, and I needed his help again. He wasn't his usual clean and crisp self, probably having hurtled here at ninety miles per hour.

"Oh, no," he said when he saw me.

"Heller! I'm so glad I found you!"

"Donohue, what the hell are you doing here?!"

"Don't you remember? You got me a flight out of Tan Son Nhut this morning to catch up with my ship in Manila? Is there still transport to the airfield?" He looked at me as if I were dumb, crazy, or suffering from shock. Maybe I *was* in shock—I couldn't believe what I had seen.

"They *have* Tan Son Nhut, man! *Don't you get it?!* Forget about Manila! Forget about your ship! Go back to your hotel!"

"I can't go back to my hotel!"

"I'm not asking you, pal, I'm telling you. Go back to your hotel—that's a direct order."

"My hotel is in Cholon," I said.

He shot back, "No, no, wait. You can't go to Cholon. The VC have Cholon!" He walked away, then stopped, and heaved a big sigh.

"All right, hold on a minute," he said, going behind a desk, grabbing a form, quickly scribbling on it, and handing it to me.

"Take this and go to one of the big hotels on Tu Do Street," he instructed. "Give it to the concierge."

I looked down, and, bearing the seal of the United States, was a voucher for a hotel stay "to be paid by the US Embassy." He had filled in my name and written the start date—January 31, 1968—but no end date. "Wow, man, how can I thank you?"

"By getting the hell outta here," he said, and left.

CHAPTER 23

BATTLE AT THE PRESIDENT'S PALACE

Two young men in civilian clothes were leaving the embassy when I was, and I asked them, "Hey, do you guys by any chance have wheels?"

One said distractedly, "Yeah. Do you need a lift?"

I figured that if I couldn't go back to *Papasan*'s, and I couldn't go to the Caravelle—where the Aussie guards probably had the steel door shut like a bear trap—I might as well go to the old colonial Continental Palace Hotel. I'd seen it open and guarded on my way to the embassy. Plus, it was like a fortress and near Notre Dame Basilica, in case I felt inspired to say my prayers.

"Well, if you're going by the Palace, I could use a ride."

"That's exactly where we're going," he said. "Jump in."

I hopped in the back. Then the guy behind the wheel said to his mate, "Get us more sidearms."

So, he went back into the consulate and, after a few minutes, reappeared holding three .45 handguns, belts, and ammo clips. He handed one to the driver and one to me. I took it—there was no time to explain myself, and they didn't ask. I figured they must be CIA. We weren't about to engage in small talk. We all put on our belts, and the driver took off as fast as hell.

He floored it all the way down the main drag, right past the old Renault—the bodies were still there. I looked up and saw a few people peeking from windows and doorways as we raced by.

He sped right past Tu Do Street, missing the turn for the hotel. When he flew around the next corner, I said, "Um, weren't you guys going to the Palace?"

He replied, "We are." And with that, he made another turn, and there was the palace that he meant: not the hotel but the Presidential Palace, South Vietnam's White House. All of a sudden, *boom!* A rocket hit the jeep speeding ahead of us, the only other vehicle in sight. The jeep launched into the air, with people flying out of it in every direction.

In a second, my two guys jumped out of our jeep—one to the left and one to the right—and tore off running. The jeep kept rolling forward, and I bailed out with my head down. I ran behind another one of those giant palms. There was gunfire, but a soldier in an ROK uniform and as big as John Wayne ran right through it to the first jeep. He grabbed one of the wounded men from the ground, picked him up, and ran, carrying him down the block and through a door in a wall. I learned later it was the residence of the Korean ambassador. The guard left the other bodies in the street. They weren't moving.

I looked up behind me to see where the gunfire was coming from. The Vietcong had manned a concrete-and-rebar framework of a building under construction, about five stories tall.

Armed with machine guns and bazookas, they were launching rockets at the Presidential Palace guards, who were returning fire. It came out later that the VC were thirteen sappers, including a woman, who had been driven from the palace and had holed up in there. I noticed an indentation in the cement wall behind me, and I ran to it and wedged myself inside.

I could see that about thirty yards up, a young MP was lying on the sidewalk. He was a big kid who still had his baby fat on him. I wanted to check on him, but I was afraid the palace guards would mistake me for the enemy and send some unfriendly fire my way. But I couldn't let him lie there.

I got down and was inching low along the wall when suddenly I heard a voice that nearly scared me out of my shoes. "Get back!" a man hissed in a hoarse whisper. "Forget it. He's dead. I checked him."

I looked, and it was another guy I hadn't even seen lying in the street, wounded. He was dressed in plain clothes but had a .45. He said in a low voice, "I'm okay; stay back."

I jumped back into the crook in the wall. From there, I could look inside the palace gate and see the white-shirted South Vietnamese National Police and regular South Vietnamese army (ARVN) soldiers on the grounds. They were in the middle of a big argument with some US Army officers.

Then the ground began to tremble, and three US tanks started rolling down the street. The ARVN and the US Army officers ran out to meet them. Then they started yelling at each other again while the American soldiers ran under fire to tend to the wounded guy in civvies, slumped on the street.

They didn't see me, but I was about twenty feet away. The gist of it, from what I could hear, was that the American officers wanted to blow down the wall I was standing in front of and go after the VC. But the ARVN and the South Vietnamese cops wanted the Americans to get the hell out of there. They had been handed responsibility for the security of Saigon only a month before. They had this, they said in English; they could protect their President Thieu without US help. My thought bubble was, *They're doing a helluva job so far!*

An exasperated US Army lieutenant shouted at the South Vietnamese officers, "You don't need our help, huh?! Fine with me; we'll go help someone who does!"

He signaled to the tank drivers to continue down the block, and they headed out. They were followed by jeeps full of the wounded, including the guy who'd warned me to stay back. The dead were left where they had fallen. I found out later that they took the wounded to the Seventeenth Field Hospital, itself under attack by the Vietcong.

I thought that maybe I should try to go with them. But then I said to myself, *Nah, they're slightly busy right now, and they don't give a damn about me, nor should they.* They were looking for Charlie; I was trying to run away from Charlie.

Then a bunch of the South Vietnamese cops came out with M16s. They had no idea I was wedged in the wall. An American was with them—I guess he was an adviser, as he was wearing some kind of American police insignia. US police, sheriffs, and troopers had all served in Vietnam as advisers since the 1950s to train the South Vietnamese police. President Kennedy stepped up the American adviser program after paramilitary forces, led by Ngo Dinh Nhu, the younger brother of then president Ngo Dinh Diem, shot and killed eight children and a woman at a march protesting the Catholic regime's treatment of the Buddhist majority in June 1963. Then a Buddhist monk, Thich Quang Duc, self-immolated in a Saigon intersection in protest, and Ngo Dinh Nhu's haughty wife, Madame Nhu, contemptuously called it "a barbecue." Ngo Dinh Nhu's men then stole the holy man's charred heart from the altar of a Buddhist temple. Ngo Dinh Nhu and his brother, President Diem, were assassinated the following November, three weeks before President Kennedy.

The American cop in front of me was yelling at the White Shirts in a north-midwestern accent—maybe from Minnesota or Wisconsin. His interpreter explained that he wanted a ladder to be put up against a ledge of the building. The American hollered, "Let's get the hell in there and take them out!"

Now, I don't speak Vietnamese, but I didn't need a translator to tell me that these guys didn't like that idea very much. They bristled with fear. White Mice, indeed.

"Come on! What the hell is wrong with you? We've got to clear the building!"

They didn't move.

"We'll put up some smoke, and we'll scramble up there while the rest of you provide cover. Let's go, goddamn it!"

The interpreter yelled his translation, probably with the expletives included, but the White Mice just stood there, shaking their heads.

Finally, the American cop yelled, "Goddamn it, get me a f—ing ladder, and I'll do it!"

The South Vietnamese policemen liked the sound of that better. They scampered into the palace grounds and ran back with an extension ladder. The VC were trying to pick them off all along the way. The South Vietnamese cops threw smoke bombs up, and the place erupted with gunfire, but the American cop raced up the ladder and over the wall.

Within a second or so, *boom!* He came flying out backward and hit the ground. The man was out cold, but, thankfully, he must have been alive, because the Vietnamese picked him up and ran yelling down the street. They threw him into the back of a pickup truck, jumped in with him, and sped off under fire.

After that, nobody else came out from the palace grounds into the street. I stayed in that crook in the wall for what seemed an eternity as the firefight between the palace guards and the guerrillas in the construction site continued. It was to last fifteen hours. The South Vietnamese president, Nguyen van Thieu, wasn't even inside the palace: he was safely at his mother-in-law's house for New Year's down in My Thoi in the Mekong Delta, an hour and a half away. Man, had he missed all the clues. Or maybe he hadn't.

CHAPTER 24

AM I DEAD AND
IN PURGATORY?

The sun was starting to set. I had no idea how much of Saigon the VC had overrun. I didn't think I could make it that far.

I started crawling along the wall, away from the palace. I came upon a door and reached up and tried it; it was locked tight. Same thing with the next building. I made it to the corner and slid around, and there in front of me was the wide-open door to a regular apartment building. I stepped in, and the lobby was empty. I tried to lock the front door behind me, but the lock was broken. I got inside an interior door and was able to lock that.

I was inside a hallway. I couldn't find a light, and it was pitch black in there. I sat under the stairs and waited in the dark. And waited. Nobody came in or out the whole night. Everyone had probably fled the building. As much as I could sense, nothing moved past the front of it: not a car, not a truck, not a person. I still had the .45 and seven bullets, and if somebody would have walked through that door, I think I would have shot him.

You know, back in New York, people will tell you, "Chickie knows everybody." They're not necessarily all friends, and, thank God, I do have a lot of friends, but I kinda know everybody. I'm a communicative guy.

But here I was, after watching people being killed, and I didn't know a soul. Worse, nobody knew me. Our servicemen couldn't help me; they had their own problems. I was invisible. They had no time for me, and I don't blame them. I would have been doing the same thing. It wasn't like the Vietnamese cops could help me, either—they were trying to help their own country. There was no one to talk to. For the first time in my life, I was alone. I'd never known that feeling before, and it didn't feel good.

I don't know if I was drifting in and out of sleep or was woozy from hunger or if I went temporarily crazy, but after hours alone and on alert in the darkness, I started to see and hear things.

"Chickie, c'mon, gimme two more eggs!"

"No, man, Chuckles, you missed last time—how can you miss the Circle Line boat? Anyway, I only have four left."

"C'mon, just one, then!"

Chuckles and I were up inside the blue trestle of the Henry Hudson Bridge, egg bombing the day liners sliding through Spuyten Duyvil Creek. It was a little cooler up on the bridge on this scorcher of a July day, but not much, so as soon as Chuckles hit a guy in a hat—and you could see from his body language how miffed he was about that—it was time to celebrate.

We scrambled across to the cliffs on the Bronx side of the bridge. It would be a while before the current shifted back toward Inwood and we could ride it, praying that the time wouldn't coincide with sewage being blasted into the creek—which would send us diving like mad under it.

"I'm gonna jump off Big C!" yelled Ricky Duggan. A giant blue C, for Columbia University, was painted on the highest cliff, which towered ninety feet above the water. "Me, too!" chimed in Tommy Collins.

"No way!" I shouted. "If you get killed on my watch, then your mother and my mother will kill me—twice."

I made my way up Big Boy, as we called it. I took one long look at the Palisades across in New Jersey, where my father was selling hot dogs under the roller coaster in Palisades Park. He would do that all day, then work as a janitor in the Faber pen factory in Englewood, New Jersey, at night. I also gazed at Manhattan, at our beloved Inwood Park, still lush with the same virgin forest that shaded the Lenape Indians before they "sold" their island to Peter Minuit, the Dutch director general of the colony of New Netherlands, under their sacred tulip tree there, in 1626. The blue expanse below was clear of boats. Tarzan pose, push off, jump, and then I was falling, falling, falling, and splash! Blackness.

I snapped to.

I wasn't in the cool waters of the Spuyten Duyvil. I was still in a godforsaken hallway in the middle of Saigon that was as hot as a Russian steam bath on the Lower East Side. I went to the door, and I still could hear shots from a couple of blocks away. I started pacing.

"Hey, kid! You skylarkin' over there? I called you!"

I stopped sweeping the floor of the Dyckman Democratic Club that my aunt Florence ran. I dashed over to where the judge was playing poker with some political operatives who were regulars at the club.

"Chickie, run up to Bennie's and get me a cigar, will ya? No, two. I have a feeling this is going to be a l-o-n-g game." All the men laughed knowingly.

I knew he wasn't talking about a straight flush beating a full house.

The game they were really playing was getting their preferred candidates elected, or rewarding local lawyers with judgeships because they'd done them a lot of favors, such as getting their relatives out of jams.

"Yeah, pick up a new pack of cards, too, Chickie."

"And a cream soda."

"And a Clark bar, kid."

"Pepsi."

"Too bad he can't buy beer!" More laughter.

"Well, if we get O'Connell elected, let's make him introduce a bill that says kids can buy beer with a note from their parents." Even louder laughter.

"Maybe he should run on that platform! That'd get the votes!" Raucous laughter now.

They all gave me different wads of bills, but they knew I would keep it all straight. The judge slipped me a ten, and I was glad—he was a big tipper.

I opened the door, the Saturday sunlight flooded into the dark club, and off I ran to Bennie's on the corner. I picked up Macanudo cigars, and a deck of blue-backed Bicycle cards. I ran back into the darkness of the club, handed out the spoils and the change, and when I reached the judge, I heard the magic words: "Keep it, Chickie."

"Thanks a lot, Your Honor!" I said in earnest, and the guys got a big belly laugh out of that. Their laughter echoed in the darkness, and I heard my aunt call out over it:

"Time to go home, Chickie! Your mother wants you to come home. Go on home, now. Go on home."

I woke up either from a dream or a hallucination and I thought, *Hey, you can't drift off, man! If the Vietcong are inside my embassy grounds, pissing on the plants, then they're everywhere. Keep it together!*

I was sitting against the wall in the gloom. There was nothing to see or hear.

It was then that I thought . . . I actually might have died.

I thought I might have been shot in front of the embassy like the others there; that I had died instantly behind that tree, because I didn't remember being wounded. I thought I might be dead, and I wondered how my family would take it. I fell deep in thought, and I went back to my Catholicism, my religious training, and I believed then that I must be in purgatory.

In Catholic school, they told elaborate stories about hell and about heaven. They even talked about limbo, where they said unbaptized infants and upstanding non-Catholics went, so I always pictured Abraham Lincoln floating around with babies in limbo. But they never really described purgatory to a tee.

What if this solitude were my purgatory? A place where I never talked to anybody and nobody talked to me. Where I grew up, everybody knew everybody, and I knew everybody. I couldn't go a block without seeing or talking to somebody I knew. Even here, in a war zone, I had run into people I knew. But now, maybe for the first time I could remember, I was completely alone for a sustained period. It felt like . . . death.

It was that, and the fear of the unknown. The fear of what was outside the door. What was going on? Maybe the VC would come through that door. I was preparing for that eventuality.

Still, you don't have time for fear in a situation like that. You'd better have your wits about you. What do I mean by that? Don't do something stupid. Don't walk out in the middle of the street, look around, and say, "Hey! Is there anybody around?!" Because there is, and they might not like you.

CHAPTER 25

BEFRIENDING A SOUTH VIETNAMESE COP

After I don't know how many hours, the sunlight filtered through a crack in the door. A spider scurried across it. I got up and ventured out. I looked up and down the street; it was empty and quiet. So, I staggered along the buildings up to Tu Do Street. You could still hear gunfire across the city, and a fleet of choppers was overhead. A lot of South Vietnamese cops were out now, but, still, very few people and virtually no vehicles were navigating the streets.

I was just wandering about, having completely given up any thought of getting to my ship. I assumed I was dead. It didn't matter.

It was then that I heard, "Ay, Chickie!"

I looked up. It was Martin, one of the seamen from the SS *Limon*.

I asked him, "Hey, man . . . Are you alive?"

"Whaddaya mean?! What are you talking about?"

"We're both alive?"

"Chick, are you all right?" Martin asked, and in his expression, you could see he thought I was crazy. "Why don't you come back with me to the *Limon*, and we'll see Johnny."

"You're the first guy I've seen in days that I know, man!" I told him. I was so happy. "I'm glad we're alive!"

"Yeah! We're alive!" Martin said, and he slapped me on the back, but he looked worried. He tried to convince me to come back to the ship with him, and I thanked him and told him to say hello to my old merchant marine friend Johnny Jackson. But I had to head on my way.

By now, it was a certainty that my second ship had sailed, so I had to hunker down and find a plan C. I hiked into the next neighborhood and went up to a South Vietnamese cop standing in the middle of the street. I asked him the status of Cholon, where my hotel was. There had been house-to-house fighting there with VC who were operating out of the Phu Tho racetrack they'd overtaken. Houses were bombed out. Blocks of Cholon would end up shelled flat—maybe in a thousand-year-old vendetta against Chinese oppression, but, ironically, probably carried out with Chinese-made rockets.

"VC are still all over the place in Cholon," he said in almost flawless English.

I said, "I need to find a hotel." He looked at me skeptically like, um, tourist season is over, buddy.

But I told him my story (the abridged version) and showed him the hotel voucher I'd gotten from the embassy on a day that seemed so long ago now. He nodded and seemed to be okay with it.

"You see that?" he asked, pointing to a small building across the street. "That's my father's hotel."

He had obviously posted himself there to guard his father and probably the rest of his family. It looked like a no-tell motel—you know, where a couple might go for an hour or so. I didn't care. I needed to regroup, perhaps for a night, two at the most, before I finally got out of town.

"Do you have any vacancies?" I asked, and at that, he gave me a look. We both burst into laughter. The whole place was empty. It was the first laugh I'd had in days, and it was probably the same with him. Nuong was his name, and we would become friends. I gave him the voucher, he brought me in, his father gave me a room, and I hit the pillow and slept. I hadn't gotten much sleep in that vestibule. You don't need sleep when you're dead.

CHAPTER 26

A GIANT FLOATING
FREEZER FULL OF FOOD
IN THE MIDST OF FAMINE

US military forces had regained control of the American embassy within six hours, and the South Vietnamese had regained President Thieu's palace by the next day. But the Vietcong still controlled cities all over the country, and they still had the airport outside Saigon and some sections of the capital. In the ensuing days, the city was shut down. You'd hear sporadic gunfire during the night. There were refugees in the streets. Garbage was piling up.

Worst of all, there was no food. Saigon wasn't getting any truck deliveries, and the port was closed. Word was that the longshoremen were Communist sympathizers, and so they had called a phony strike to stop supplies from getting in. They must have paid off the corrupt South Vietnamese officials, if that's not redundant.

The city was blockaded. Nuong's father didn't have any food at his little grey hotel, so I soon used it as a place to sleep and would forage for food at the bigger hotels serving the Western press. I found food, and kindred spirits, at the bar on top of the Caravelle Hotel. But as the Tet offensive raged on through February, they ran out of food everywhere. All they had at the Caravelle was rice and a few vegetables, and, occasionally, some shrimp.

But because the port was shut down, the SS *Limon,* Johnny's ship, was still loaded and anchored in the river. It was filled to the brim with frozen spareribs and hams, and I was having visions of hamburgers, like the burger-obsessed moocher Wimpy in the *Popeye* cartoons. Even though the port was closed, I headed down there because, to paraphrase bank robber Willie Sutton, that's where the grub was.

The dock was heavily guarded, but I casually flashed my seaman's ID and barely slowed down. The White Shirts stopped me, looked at the card, looked at me, and waved me on.

I got to the ship and asked for Johnny. He came to the gangway and took a hard look at me. "You all right, Chickie?" I guess his mate had filled him in.

"I'm okay, I'm okay. A little hungry is all."

Johnny brought me right down to the galley, where we had eaten before, and he and the seamen gave me another big feed: barbecued chicken, corn on the cob, baked potatoes. I don't think food has tasted as delicious to me before or since. They had plenty of it, and they sat there happily watching me chow down. They had nothing else to do. Johnny and the other mariners of the *SS Limon* had orders to remain on ship. The captain was not being overcautious: two seamen from the SS *Express Baltimore* had disembarked to find their captain in Da Nang a couple of years before, when orders came down to ship out. They never came back. And a young merchant mariner from the SS *Columbia Banker,* Michael C. Miller, had been killed in front of the American embassy the very day I was there hiding behind the palm tree. Maybe he was one of the ones I saw taken away by the soldiers in the jeep, I don't know.

It wasn't any safer on the ship. Johnny and the other mariners were targets on the *Limon,* which I felt was one big bull's-eye at the dock. On August 26, 1966, another merchant marine Victory ship like the *Limon,* the SS *Baton Rouge,* was sailing to Saigon on the Long Tau River up from the coast, when a mine blasted a forty-five-foot hole in it. The entire seven-man engine crew of mariners was killed.

I tried to keep the seamen entertained and finally thanked them profusely and got up to go. I said to them, "Listen, there's nothing moving in Saigon. The stores are shut down, and there's no food in the hotels. Do you mind if I bring some food back to the guys who work at the Caravelle bar?"

No problem, they said. What the hell did they care? They had tons of food, and for all they knew, they'd have to bring it all back to Manila if the Tet offensive went on and on. So, they loaded me up with a big duffel bag bulging with burgers, whole chickens, and corn on the cob. They snuck me out when the chief mate wasn't looking. By the time I passed security, the guards had changed shift, so I showed them my US passport. I would go back and forth: seaman's documents to enter the port, and a US passport stamped "US Embassy Saigon" to leave.

At the Caravelle bar, I walked over to the manager, clutching my bag of contraband.

"Come back into the kitchen with me," I said with a smile.

When we got to the steel table, I dumped it all out, and a cry went up. The manager said I was like Santa with his big bag of presents on his back. The chefs and the bartender, they all scrambled and grabbed the stuff and immediately started cooking it—not for the guests but for themselves. The chefs were *starving*. I told them that if any seamen from the SS *Limon* were to come in, drinks were on the house.

Out front, the journalists were shaking their heads over President Thieu's announcement that he would institute a military draft for eighteen- and nineteen-year-olds. They felt bad for these kids, as they did for our own, of course, but were incredulous that conscription hadn't been in place already, given that American boys had been drafted into the Vietnam War since 1965.

I kept checking in at the US consulate each day to see if I could board any ships headed back to the States. I would have worked free to pay for passage, but nothing was moving. Then I would go to the French shipping agent's house. I never saw him again. Mr. Minh, his gentlemanly servant, said he had gone to the country, and I thought, *Which one? Bali? France?* I'd stay and talk to Mr. Minh, who was probably more educated than his boss, and after a while, he would give me a couple days' advance on the money.

I went back to the *Limon* each day and hung out with the guys; they felt trapped on the ship. I gave them reports from the outside world and told them the different ways the chefs—some of them French trained—had prepared their cuisine. Then, like Santa's elves, they'd load me up, and off I'd go. They'd think of all kinds of ways to sneak me and this cornucopia past the captain and off the ship. They liked doing something of value instead of twiddling their thumbs.

I soon started bringing food to my friends such as Nuong, the South Vietnamese cop, and his father, who owned the little hotel where I was living. They started divvying it up with their relatives and children, and then their neighbors started showing up with *their* children. I will never forget the looks of joy on those kids' faces when they were served *vegetables*. I tried to remember to stash cookies in the bag on future trips.

When it was too hot to sleep, Nuong and I would sit out back, and he'd have a little dinner, and we'd talk politics into the wee hours. He told me about the long, sad history of his country, including about 1,800 years of Chinese domination, its conquest in the thirteenth century by Kublai Khan at the same time that Marco Polo was in Vietnam marveling at the totally tattooed men and women of the kingdom of Tonkin. Nuong said that over the centuries, various revolutions had been attempted, like the one led by the legendary Trung sisters, Trac and Nhi, who, in AD 40, led an army of eighty thousand against the Chinese invaders. They were like Joan of Arc times two.

We Americans had stepped into a region with enmities as old as in the Middle East. Now China was supplying the North Vietnamese army with Shenyang J-6 fighter jets, Russian machine guns, Type 56 assault rifles, and Chicom stick grenades. When I told Nuong that, like myself, Ho Chi Minh had been a seaman, and he had lived and worked in Brooklyn in the early nineteen hundreds, he couldn't believe it.

Soon I was carrying two duffel bags off the ship every night. When I told the seamen on the *Limon* that even the hotel chefs were skipping meals so they could bring food home to their

Vietnamese children, like all children,
grow up fast in times of war.

kids, they doubled my load. The Caravelle chefs were feeding more and more folks each night, as word must have gotten out about their secret supply. In order to feed everybody, they became masters at stretching the ingredients I brought them by adding rice, and vegetables they were growing themselves on the roof. It was like the loaves and the fishes.

I needed to feed a Caravelle regular named Ben, whom I called Ben Hur. He said he was part Russian, part Jewish, part Asian, and part Native American: a man of the world. He spoke about seven languages, a perfect combo for doing business around the globe. Ben was a big shot at a company that was bringing computers into South Vietnam at US taxpayers' expense, and he knew a lot of connected people in Saigon. Just like I had to bribe the South Vietnamese State Department official to let me out of his country, Ben Hur had to bribe South Vietnamese government bureaucrats to accept our free gift of millions of dollars' worth of mainframes.

Ben thought nothing of it; he was used to paying graft all over the world. A cost of doing business, he reasoned. I, on the other hand, was incensed that we had to pay them to take our gifts while we were also helping them to fight their enemy. I made sure he got first dibs the next time I brought food back. Ben chose the lobster, and when he tasted it in butter sauce, I could swear his eyes welled up a little with tears. Feeding the kitchen and bar staff every night, we drank free. So, Ben and I would sit up there and talk and watch the choppers fly over the cathedral spires of Notre Dame and the old Saigon Opera House. We could hear gunfire in the distance and even hear B-52s dropping bombs. It was a lovely place to watch a war.

Looking over the horizon, I was worried about my buddies out there, where in many places the fighting was still fierce. Rick and the rest of the First Air Cav Bravo Company had been sent to attack a newly built North Vietnamese base in the hills—and that was just the beginning for him. Kevin had been sent with the Americal Division to Chu Lai, which was rocketed by the VC for a month. I had no idea where Richard Reynolds and Joey McFadden were. Tommy Collins was in Qui Nhon when the VC blew up part of the ammo dump and took over the radio station and train depot. There was street fighting everywhere.

Tommy told me later, "In the weeks before Tet, the *Mama-sans* in the villages kept telling us, 'Beaucoup VC, beaucoup VC'—many Vietcong—were coming into the area. We reported it to intel [army intelligence], but they told us it was 'unconfirmed.'

"The first night of Tet, our ambush patrol got wiped out. Then the VC killed the mayor, and they killed the tribal chieftain." They still had ethnic chiefs in Vietnam then, like the real ones filmed in Saigon for the 1958 film adaptation of Graham Greene's *The Quiet American*, starring Audie Murphy, the real-life World War II hero turned Hollywood actor.

Tommy's 127th Military Police Unit and the 93rd Military Police Battalion were ordered to fight off the VC, and one of Tommy's friends, a fellow MP, was killed trying to flush out a sniper. Tommy was sent to guard the POW camp, which was a big target for the Vietcong, who kept trying to free the prisoners. Tommy's unit had suffered a number of losses.

Yeah, I wondered what was going on with my old buddies and with their fellow soldiers I had gotten to know on my journey, out in that terrible, torn-up terrain.

CHAPTER 27

COAST GUARD BRASS:
A BIG JOB ON A BIG SHIP

One night, a coast guard officer came into the Caravelle bar, and he looked like he needed a drink.

He had three gold stripes under a shield on his sleeve, indicating his high rank. The officer was an authoritative man with a self-assured bearing, but he looked preoccupied. From what I gathered later, he had big responsibilities for the ships that were in limbo, like the SS *Limon* and the SS *US Tourist*: full yet afloat after weeks on the Saigon River, with the Vietnamese longshoremen still on strike and unwilling to unload cargo. Those ships would be highly vulnerable sitting so close to the city's shore anytime, but now, during the Tet offensive, the risk had spiked. He didn't say much about it, although he did mention that it was his first beer since Tet had begun. I couldn't believe I was drinking with a US Coast Guard lieutenant commander. Bars democratize all people.

After about an hour of talking about the war in general and our respective lives on the sea, he came around to asking me what I was doing in beautiful downtown Saigon.

"Well, Lieutenant Commander . . ."

"Call me Frank."

"Well, um, Frank, at the moment I am looking for a job."

"Is that right? What was your role on the ship?"

"I'm an oiler, but I can do a lot of jobs in the engine room."

"Do you have security clearance?"

"I do!"

I guess after talking, he had gotten to trust me, so he said, "I might have a job for you. Up in Qui Nhon."

Qui Nhon! That's where I started in Vietnam, where Tommy Collins was stationed. The commander said that a coast guard T2 oil tanker from World War II—the workhorse of the tanker fleet, able to hold nearly six million gallons—was supplying energy to the city from offshore. A very ill seaman had been medevacked out and wasn't going to recover quickly, he added. This tanker wasn't leaving, as it provided energy to his boats and even to coastal installations. You worked it while it was anchored in the harbor until it had to go fill up, probably in Malaysia, and come back again.*

"A job!" I said. "I'll take it!" I was picturing hanging out with Tommy Collins for the rest of his tour and having a good old time.

"You sure you're willing to risk it?" he asked. "A floating

---

* Ironically, two months before the fall of Saigon in 1975, America's Mobil Oil Corporation struck oil in the Bach Ho field after many years of expensive exploration. The Communist leadership formed a partnership with the Soviet Union called Vietsovpetro, which took over the oil field, helping to give Vietnam the four-billion-gallon oil reserve it has today.

tank of oil sitting there in the ocean is a risky place to work."

"No problem," I assured him. "My buddy and his mates are MPs there, and they do a good job."

"I don't know if you'd like the pay . . ." The commander looked at me out of the corner of his eye, and a sly smile spread across his face.

"It's union wages, isn't it?"

"Oh, it's a bit more than that," he said. "Twenty-five-hundred dollars a month."

I nearly spit out my beer.

"Twenty-five hundred a *month?!!*"

I was in disbelief. I had been earning $300 a month on the SS *Drake Victory*. This was more than eight times that!

"Oh, and there's no income tax on that," he said with a smirk, then sipped his beer. He'd been doling out the info one card at a time just to see my reaction.

"Hazard pay," he explained. "But you've got to commit to eighteen months, and you'll be sitting on the biggest liquid bomb in Vietnam."

I thought about the risk for a minute—but only for a minute. I was multiplying eighteen times $2,500 in my head: $45,000. That would equal more than $300,000 today, a life changer any way you look at it. I could buy a little tavern with that kind of dough.

He added, "I don't want to be short an oiler with six million gallons of oil in the hold."

One of the things we oilers do is keep tabs on the temperature of the generators at all times. Most ships have two generators; a T2 tanker might have ten 10,000-AV volt generators. This was basically a floating power station.

"Okay," he said. "Meet me at coast guard headquarters to-morrow at 0800 hours, and we'll reach out to them. We can fly you up to the Qui Nhon airfield tomorrow."

I thanked him profusely, said good night to my buddy Ben Hur, and looked forward to a good night's rest so I wouldn't be late. I was excited. I guess I would be staying in Vietnam for a while.

The next day, I was down at the pier by seven, content to wait. Frank came in a few minutes later. The commander was busy talking with a seaman, but he stopped when he saw me.

"Donohue!" he exulted. "Great! Let's get this done; I've got a lot on my plate today. Okay, sailor, secure a safe channel to Qui Nhon. Get me the coast guard detachment commander."

The radio operator said, "Yes, sir!" and hopped to it.

"Moby Dick for Merrimac. Moby Dick for Merrimac."

"This is Merrimac. Ensign speaking."

"You have the detachment, sir."

The commander got on the horn.

"Ensign? Let me talk to the captain. I think we got that oiler for Big Boy. I'd like to fly him up there today."

There was a pause, and then, in an urgent tone, the ensign said: "Moby Dick, do not send oiler up. Repeat, do not send oiler up."

"Why the hell not?" asked the commander.

"Charlie still has the airfield, sir. Charlie has the airfield."

The commander paused, and his jaw tensed. "Affirmative," he growled.

Now he was mad. He turned and said, "I'm sorry, Donohue, we can't do it right now. I gotta go."

They did me a favor. Had I somehow landed on that airfield, I would have become a POW—if I was lucky. I'm also glad I didn't try to make it there on my own. I knew better by now.

In my mind's eye, I saw my nice, big bag of money go up in smoke the same as if Charlie had blown it up with a rocket. Maybe it wasn't such a good idea to work on an oil tanker anchored off Vietnam right then anyway.

CHAPTER 28

AUSTRALIAN MARINES LOCK THE CARAVELLE UP TIGHT

One February night at about midnight, I realized that closing time had snuck up on me. I could hear the Australian marines pulling down the heavy steel gate over the entrance of the Caravelle Hotel for the night. This thing was massive—it shielded the entire building entrance. They have that all over the Bronx now, even on houses, but I'd never seen it before. Once it was secured, you were locked up tight, and they really didn't like opening it again. I said good night to Ben Hur and tore down in the elevator, and they let me squeak through.

"You really shouldn't go out there, mate," one said. "I'm sure they will find you a room, and if there isn't one, sleep in the lobby." The US and South Vietnamese had still not retaken Saigon: B-52s were dropping five-hundred-pound bombs all around the capital, and sporadic attacks were still being launched by the Vietcong throughout the city, especially at night.

The fighting had flared up that day. You could hear guns firing in and around Saigon and out at the Tan Son Nhut airfield. All I had to do was make it to my fleabag, which was just around the corner. Why didn't I switch the voucher to the Caravelle? Well, every day, I thought that this was the day I'd go home, or maybe land that big job on the oil tanker, so why bother? Besides, I was one of the few guests at the old man's hotel. His son, Nuong, was my friend now, and I wanted to give them the embassy-underwritten business.

It was past midnight. I passed an alley off Tu Do Street, where I had heard there was a nice little tavern, so I headed there to check it out.

I didn't get ten yards down the alley when I noticed something moving in a doorway on the left. Someone was lying in wait. I saw the weapon first: a glint off the end of the barrel of a rifle. I stopped and stood still. If I turned and ran, he could have shot me in the back. Then I realized that the height of the weapon was such that anybody holding it had to be considerably over six feet tall, a rarity among the Vietnamese.

I looked down and I saw a boot—a very big military boot—so I guessed he was American or Aussie or Kiwi—another of our allies serving there. I walked straight down the middle of the alley so he could see me clearly. I didn't want to piss him off by signaling that I had seen him. I wanted him to think he spotted me first. I could hear a squawk on his radio, and his platoon mates were on the roof and in the building. They had cast a net for somebody, and I didn't want it to be me by accident.

I sauntered down the street and started whistling before I reached the doorway.

"Halt!" he yelled. It was a young soldier with an M16 rifle.

"Hey, buddy," I said. "How are you doing? What are you doing here?"

"What the . . . What am *I* doing here?!" he said incredulously. "What the hell are *you* doing here?!"

"I'm going for a beer," I said. "I heard there's a good joint down the end of the alley."

"Are you out of your mind?" he said to me in kind of a scream-whisper. "Going for a beer? Charlie's all over the city, and you're out strolling in the middle of the street, going for a beer?!"

"Well," I said, "I'm thirsty. There's supposed to be a nice pub right at the end of this street."

"There's nothing open down this whole block, buddy," he growled.

By this point, he seemed intrigued, as if he were thinking, *What kind of awesome bar could this be that an American pops out of the mist in a war zone to find it?* So, we walked together—he's still got the M16 rifle up, pointing ahead. He couldn't have been older than eighteen or nineteen, like Tommy Collins.

We reached the end of the block, and there it was: a little colonial hideaway that looked like it had been airdropped from Paris and hadn't changed since its French clientele had fled. But it was locked tight.

"Listen, man, I don't know *who* you are or *what* your story is," he said quietly, "but you'd better leave *right now.* Where do you live?"

"Just around the corner."

"Okay, look, head there and call it a night," he advised.

So I did, and before I turned the corner, I looked over my shoulder, and the kid was covering me. I got home all right, and I hope he did, too. All the way home.

The following day, when I brought the next feed bag to the Caravelle, I organized the hotel guests into a little strike with one demand: the bar stays open past midnight. If we had to be trapped in the Tet offensive, we might at least drink. I didn't want to lose my life over it.

CHAPTER 29

FINDING BOBBY

Fighting continued in key cities and strategic military bases, most intensely in Khe Sanh and Hue, where US Marines were on the front lines.

I was worried about Richard Reynolds, the marine second lieutenant who was on my list, as I'm sure his many brothers and cousins in Inwood were, too. I didn't know where in hell he was.

He could be in Khe Sanh, a key location near the Ho Chi Minh Trail running inside the border with Laos, where five thousand leathernecks and their army support remained cut off and surrounded by twenty thousand North Vietnamese soldiers. LBJ ordered it to be held "at all costs"—a major miscalculation ten days before Tet, as anyone can see in the Stanley Kubrick film *Full Metal Jacket* or journalist Michael Herr's eyewitness account, *Dispatches*.

Or, Richie could be in Hue, the imperial city on the Perfume River thirty miles south of the DMZ near Phu Bai, where three US Marine battalions and South Vietnamese soldiers were under siege, fighting off ten battalions of Vietcong and North

Vietnamese army soldiers, while part of the US Army's First Cavalry Division battled to reach them.

At first, fighter pilots were ordered not to bomb the ancient citadel, which was akin to the Forbidden City of China, with 160 palaces and temples that General Giap's forces were using as fortresses, even as they were going house to house executing civilians. The pols didn't want it to become another Dresden, Germany, where, during the final months of World War II, more than 1,200 British and US bomber pilots destroyed the bell-domed Frauenkirche church and other Baroque landmarks and killed 25,000 people by dropping incendiary bombs which consumed 80 percent of the city in a firestorm. Kurt Vonnegut Jr., an American POW in Dresden during the bombing who wrote about later in his novel *Slaughterhouse-Five*,* was made to bury the bodies. I hoped US reinforcements would reach Khe Sanh and Hue soon and that, wherever he was, Richie would be all right. I worried about Joey McFadden, too—my friend Pally's younger brother, who was an army private. I had no idea where he was, either.

I knew exactly where Bobby Pappas was, though: at the sprawling Long Binh army base only about an hour from Saigon, near the city of Bien Hoa. Our forces had secured the main road going northeast, and I saw military transports

---

* As the battle in Hue was heading into March, we had 1,364 wounded and 216 killed. US military leaders, who had tried to preserve the heritage sites, finally decided enough was enough and ordered marine A-4 Skyhawk pilots to bomb the citadel, ending the bloody battle. By some estimates, more than 13,000 Vietnamese on both sides, including civilians executed by the NVA, had been killed, and all but about thirty of the old emperor's royal palaces had been destroyed.

rumbling in and out of town. I realized this might be a beautiful time to find Bobby. He had been my best friend and partner in crime back home. I absolutely had to bring him a New York beer and, hell, give him a great big bear hug, too.

Security would be tight, though. Bobby was a communications specialist at Long Binh, which housed the military's main ammunition supply depot—the largest in the world. Vietcong sappers had blown up fifteen thousand 155-millimeter artillery missiles at the "ammo dump" the year before, and it took two months to dig up and safely remove the undetonated ones.

Now, with the Tet offensive continuing, it was a tinderbox.

I checked in with the shipping agent's clerk, Mr. Minh, and told him I would be upcountry for a couple of days. By this point, we were friends, so he didn't think anything of bending the rules and giving me three days' pay in advance.

Back out on the road, I hitched a ride northeast to the Long Binh base. When we arrived, I couldn't believe the huge scale of the place. About fifty thousand soldiers were stationed there, as well as some of the top army generals in charge of planning the logistics of the war. Long Binh had restaurants, stores, an Olympic-size swimming pool, tennis courts, basketball courts, a golf driving range, a bowling alley, classrooms, theaters, tennis courts, and nightclubs. Bob Hope had brought his Christmas show there, entertaining the troops, while in the front row, General Westmoreland, Ambassador Bunker, and South Vietnamese vice president Nguyen Cao Ky sat watching Raquel Welch do the frug.

I walked to the depot outside the base. They had to keep it far from all the personnel in case anything happened. There were artillery and mountains of ammunition crates, mortars of all sizes, organized row after row, like pyramids of pyrotechnics. The front gate of the ammo depot was heavily guarded. I sauntered up to the MPs and showed them my seaman documents and my shiny new Saigon-issued passport. I told them Bobby Pappas was my stepbrother.

"Oh, yeah?" said one MP. "Tell us a Pappas story, then. One of those outlandish New York stories he's always telling that we're supposed to believe."

"You mean like the one about the crazy guy who followed us everywhere? And one day he followed us into a supermarket on Dyckman Street, and we handed him a package of chopped beef, and he ran through the aisles with it over his head, screaming, 'Chuck chop! Chuck chop!' and that became his nickname?"

They looked at each other wide eyed, and one said, "All right, hop in the jeep. I'll drive you in myself."

When we got to the underground communications bunker, the driver told the MPs guarding it that I was Bobby's stepbrother trying to visit him while my ship was in port. One MP went down and told Bobby that somebody was there to see him, but he didn't say who. Then they let me go down. Bobby was there with two other guys, operating all the main communications equipment for the depot.

I said casually, "Hey, buddy."

Bobby turned and bellowed, "Chick?!" He looked at me for a long minute as if he couldn't process it. "What the hell are you doing here?" My friend looked different: military neat.

"I'm here to see you, man!" I gave him a big hug. "Also to bring you a beer, from all the gang back home. We got together and decided we wanted to show you guys from the neighborhood over here that we appreciate what you're doing."

I reached in my pack and handed him a can of the good stuff, and gave out some to the other guys.

"I see my gesture is a bit symbolic—you've got bars all over the base!" I said.

"Yeah, but we don't always have these brands. Anyway, that's exactly where we're headed after we have these. But first I have to finish my shift!"

I sat with Bobby as he worked, and we caught up. I gave him news of his wife and kid and his dad and folks we knew back in New York. I told him what I had seen in Saigon on the first night of Tet, and about the CIA Effect that had gotten me through the country. Then the next shift of communications guys came to relieve Bobby and his mates.

"Let's go," said Bobby. "But first we've got to stop at my tent, so I can give you my extra fatigues."

We did that, and Bobby even took me to the PX, the post exchange on-base store. I was the only US civilian I could see on the base, and Bobby didn't want to explain me to every inquiring mind.

"Hey, can I get a fatigues jacket for my compadre here? He came all the way from New York to see me."

"No problem, Sergeant," replied the corporal behind the counter. "Name?"

"Chick Donohue," said Bobby, and he spelled it out. The guy stenciled it on. "What do I put on the right? I can't put 'US Army.'"

Bobby looked at me and laughed. "Print 'Civilian,'" he said. I pulled it on.

"So how are you really doing, man?" I asked Bobby.

"Well, I hope I make it back in time to hear my son say 'Dada.'"

"Yeah, it sucks that LBJ reneged on JFK's promise to leave fathers out of this. But at least you're stationed at a base," I offered.

"Hey, I'm grateful for that," he said. "But I'd be a liar if I said the ammo dump next door didn't spook me every so often. It's about twenty-two hundred acres big, and we're surrounded by jungle on three sides. We have everything in the depot: howitzer shells, rockets, flares, hand grenades, mortars—every kind of munitions, we have cases and cases of them.

"We do have thirty-two watchtowers all around the pe-rimeter, and, of course, guards constantly patrolling on the ground. They watch for sappers who would cut a hole in the fence in the dark and then get in and blow up the pads.

"The VC have such a jones for it. All they need to do is detonate one missile in the pile, and the whole thing blows. They've already done it two years in a row." He pointed off into the distance. "And about six miles away is Bien Hoa Air Base, which also has a major bull's-eye on it. It's home to the air force's Third Tactical Fighter Wing, so they have a lot of jets on the airfield, and it's home to the army's 145th Aviation Battalion helicopter unit, and navy and marine units as well. It's where most of our troops first came in. It's a major target like we are."

I shook my head. He asked if I was hungry.

"Let's head over to the enlisted men's club," he said. Bobby was a sergeant, but he had been drafted and wouldn't

I found my buddy Sgt. Bobby Pappas at the communications bunker at the Long Binh ammunition depot, the biggest in the world, and a target for Vietcong sappers. Pappas brought me to the PX and bought me a fatigue jacket to cover the by-now iconic, not to mention well-worn, madras shirt. The stencil on my right read "Chick Donohue" and the stencil on my left, instead of US Army, read "Civilian".

ordinarily be allowed in the club. "The officers knew I had been a bartender in New York, so whenever they have parties, I tend bar for them for extra money. They always let me eat what they're eating, too, like shrimp and beef, which sure beats C-rations. Maybe they'll see this is a special occasion."

They did. They let us in, and we sat at the bar among the officers, including Bobby's commanding officer, who was at a nearby table. After a while, I guess in our comfort zone, Bobby and I were swearing as if we were back on the streets. The CO became visibly perturbed.

"Chick, you have to watch your mouth," Bobby told me. "My CO is a devout Mormon. He even wears the temple garments under his uniform in this heat. He's a nice man, and he treats everybody fairly, but he hates it when we curse. When my company captain told him he was thinking of promoting me to sergeant, the CO told me, 'Pappas, you are the most foulmouthed person I have ever met in my life, and you have exhibited a great deal of belligerence at times. Therefore, you would make a great sergeant. I approve.'"

As if on cue, the CO appeared behind us at the bar.

"Sergeant Pappas, I see you have found a drinking partner who is as foulmouthed as yourself," he said, peering down at my jacket. "'Chick Donohue' . . . 'civilian'?"

Bobby quickly intervened. "Sir, this is my friend here to visit me while his ship is in port. He was at the embassy during the fight to take it back."

The CO pulled up a stool. He wanted to know all the military details, how our forces had handled the situation— whatever I knew. He had one question after the next and forgot all about the cursing.

"Sir, I think the war is essentially over," I ventured. "This was the North Vietnamese army's last shot, and we won. They've got to come to the peace table now and start negotiating."

He seemed happy with that, but I wasn't sure that even I believed it. I mostly wanted to reassure Bobby, who wanted to return to his family.

I stayed in a spare bunk that night and hung out with my pal the next day in the communications bunker. The following night, we went to the regular GIs' bar to hang out with Bobby's best friends on campus. They were sergeants, too. One was from Fresno, California; the other from someplace in Nebraska.

"Can I ask you something, Chick?" said the one from Nebraska. "Is Pappas full of s—, or is he in the Mafia, or what, because his stories are not to be believed."

"Like what?" I asked.

"Like, did you two let somebody stay in your apartment because he had worn out his welcome everywhere else, then he got hot so he broke every single window in the apartment, but then it became freezing, so you two went to a bar because it'd be warmer? And when you came home, firefighters were putting out a fire he set because he was cold?"

"One hundred percent true," I confirmed. "That would be Jimbo. Jimbo was crazy, but not in the Mafia. Now, Mikey, *he* was in the Mafia."

We told more stories, drank beer, and had a lot of laughs. I stayed another couple of nights in his barracks, but then it was time for me to go.

"Well, Bobby," I told him, "unless your CO wants to give me a job for twenty-five hundred a month like the coast guard commander does or fly me home on General Westmoreland's plane, I have to go back to Saigon and get sorted out. Besides, you've got your own job to do."

He nodded. "Yeah, man. I'll be back in a couple of months, and if you beat me home, we'll celebrate with Jimbo and Chuck Chop at the Colonel's!"

"You got it," I said, and he reached out to shake my hand. I took it and then grabbed both of his shoulders and gave him a good shake.

"See ya' at Doc Fiddler's."

CHAPTER 30

EXPLOSION AT LONG BINH

The night I got back from visiting Bobby Pappas, I went up to the rooftop bar at the Caravelle. There was the usual crowd of reporters, businessmen, officers, and the random misfits stuck in Saigon, like me and Ben Hur.

Many of the correspondents were complaining about the official daily press conference at the Rex Hotel, which they'd started to call the "Five O'Clock Follies," and from which they'd give Ben Hur and me the headlines each day. They weren't exactly objective about it. They especially hated Thursdays, when the US press spokesman would state the body counts, with the NVA and VC always having higher casualties, and us "winning" the "score."

They didn't seem to respect Westmoreland, especially since he'd showed up at the embassy "in his crisp, clean uniform," as Don North of ABC News put it, minutes after the heroic young MPs and marines had retaken it and before the reporters arrived, to whom he declared: "The enemy's plans have run afoul."

One reporter griped, "Westmoreland is asking for two hundred six thousand more boys to be sent over! Meanwhile, the Senate is holding hearings to determine whether the Gulf of Tonkin incident that started the war even happened." On August 2, 1964, the destroyer USS *Maddox* was in international waters off the coast of North Vietnam, yet close to Hon Me Island in the Gulf of Tonkin when three North Vietnamese P-4 torpedo boats manned by three brothers and North Vietnamese navy sailors approached. Captain John J. Herrick of the USS *Maddox* ordered its gunners to fire warning shots first. The NVN sailors fired back with torpedoes and machine guns; four Vought F-8 Crusaders then took off from the nearby USS *Ticonderoga* and attacked them as they headed back to shore. Ten NVN sailors were hit; four died; the USS *Maddox* sustained only a single bullethole. On August 4, USS *Maddox* sailors monitoring their radar and sonar in bad weather thought they picked up signs of imminent attack by NVN torpedo boats and the perceived boats were fired upon. Captain Herrick later cabled Washington that the signals were probably caused by rough seas and the weather and not actual boats. But that was enough for President Johnson and the US Congress, which five days later passed the Gulf of Tonkin resolution giving LBJ the power to unilaterally order military action. By February 1965, his Operation Rolling Thunder planes were carpet-bombing North Vietnam.

Another added, "Westmoreland and LBJ still believe the whole Tet offensive is a diversionary tactic to distract them from Khe Sanh in the North! It's the exact opposite! LBJ says he doesn't want Khe Sanh to be his Dien Bien Phu, and he can't even pronounce it!"

Dien Bien Phu was the site of a decisive victory by the Vietnamese Communists, led by Ho Chi Minh, over the French in

1954. The defeat in what is known as the First Indochina War (1946–1954) led France to withdraw from Vietnam, Cambodia, and Laos (Indochina) after nearly a hundred years of colonial rule, and Vietnam was split in half at the 17th parallel after the Geneva Accords, with the Communists controlling the north, leaving us where we were today.

"Can they really believe that General Giap put the whole country under siege to take attention away from one border spot?!" another journo wailed. I didn't have an answer for him.

Journalists covering Vietnam exerted a lot more influence than even Edward R. Murrow had during the Second World War. Pundits called the conflict in Vietnam a "television" war. The speed with which reporters could deliver their stories to the papers or on the air back home added to their influence. The Associated Press and other wire services and big newspapers were now able to transmit reporters' updates within seconds on teletype machines. NBC's Saigon Bureau television crews would pass their footage to staffers on medevac flights flying to Yokota Air Force Base, six hours away in Japan. Then network staffers at the Tokyo Bureau met the plane, grabbed the footage, rented time on a communications satellite, and had it on the evening TV news twenty-four hours after the fact: vivid, powerful footage of the embassy takeover and other Tet battles.

The members of the press were arguing with one another, when suddenly there was a gigantic explosion about twenty miles away to the northeast. Some people who'd been on the street said they felt the impact through their shoes. It shook the whole city of Bien Hoa, six miles away. The night sky lit up orange, and a huge mushroom cloud rose, like an atomic bomb. Some soldiers there thought the NVA had gotten hold of a nuclear weapon. This set off a chain reaction of fireworks that got bigger and bigger—*boom! Boom! BOOM!*—as VC satchel charges blew up and entire pallets of artillery ammunition ignited. With each successive explosion, I knew it had to be Long Binh, and Bobby Pappas was in the middle of it all.

The correspondents tore out of there to find out what the hell happened, and I prayed. I hoped to God that Bobby was in his bunker under the ground, but I didn't see how he and the other guys could escape harm in such a conflagration. I had to go there and check if he was alive and all right. I tried, but I couldn't make it there that night. At my hotel, I couldn't sleep, resolving that if the worst had happened, I would accompany his body back to New York. But how would I break the news to his wife? Jeez, they had a baby. It was not a good night.

At first light, I hustled up with a convoy that was speeding straight to Long Binh on Highway 1A, the long spine of Vietnam that the French had built from the southern tip at Nam Can to China, 1,400 miles north. Along the way, we saw refugees hurrying south and military trucks and ambulances speeding north. Besides Long Binh, the VC had also blown up the fuel tanks at Bien Hoa airfield six miles north, pounding it with rockets and mortars.

As Bobby had explained, Bien Hoa was a huge, strategically key air base; home not only to the Air Force's Third Tactical Fighter Wing but also the army's 145th Aviation Battalion, and navy and marine units as well. More than five hundred supersonic F-100 Super Sabres and other fighter jets, Hueys, and AH-1 Cobra gunships filled the tarmac. General Giap knew he could cripple air support of our combatants on the ground, not to mention our bombing of North Vietnam, if he could obliterate the airfield. There were rumors that he himself was running the Tet offensive out of a church in Bien Hoa. Since the base also served the South Vietnamese Air Force, I could see Giap getting extra pleasure out of that.

Chopper pilots had managed to lift off, and they were still engaged in a firefight with the Vietcong entrenched at the base of the airfield. Fighter pilots, however, were stymied by the tons of shrapnel and debris scattered all over the tarmac. Under fire, airmen and GIs cleared one runway, and the F-100 pilots took off, circled, and starting bombing Bien Hoa airfield. It's believed to be the first time that US pilots performed an airstrike on their own base.

We arrived at Long Binh, and the truck stopped at the gate. One of the GIs whom Bobby and I had hung out with was on guard. I was relieved to see him alive. Maybe it was a good sign, I thought.

The Long Binh base, where most of the soldiers resided, was on one side of Highway 1A, and on the other side stood the ammunition depot. I walked over, not knowing what to expect, and nervous. Inside the depot, the place was a wreck. There were huge bombshells, some detonated, some not, strewn for acres, looking eerily like piles of bodies. Concertina wire dangled like birthday ribbons, and buildings stood charred and in ruins, as soldiers were working fast to rebuild downed guard towers. The communications bunker was right in the center of it all. I walked in and—I'll never forget it—amidst all the chaos, there was Bobby, with not a smudge on him. He had survived the night in the bunker with two or three other guys.

Instead of a smile and a hug, he gave me one look and started ranting and raving:

"You son of a ***&&%%##! You said this freakin' war was over! Look at this place! Does it look like this freakin' war is over?!"

I was so happy to see my friend safe, sound, and normal. He's pissed off at me? That's great. I knew he was okay. I thought, *Here's my Bobby—there's nothing wrong with this guy.*

"Bobby," I said, "can't you take a joke?"

He shook his head and laughed.

I *had* believed that we were winning, because I'd believed what our leaders were saying, and I wanted Bobby to feel better about where he was. But our leaders had told us Charlie was losing the war. Then they pop up all over the country? Tet changed everything.

He was as glad to see me as I was to see him. Bobby proceeded to tell me what happened.

"At around three o'clock in the morning, I needed a cigarette, so I went out of the bunker. I looked over, and I saw the rockets go into the air base. The rockets—they looked like shooting stars—they must have hit some munitions or a fuel tank, because I saw a couple of big fireballs, and I said, 'Oh boy, we're gonna get it next.' Sure as s—, we took a couple of rockets in the depot, but nothing blew up that time."

He took a breath and continued: "I got a call on my radio saying that the Long Binh ammunition depot and Bien Hoa Air Base were going on alert as of midnight. It wasn't the highest alert; it was the second highest. They had intel that something big was going to happen, but I don't think they were expecting anything like what happened. There was supposed to be a truce, but General Giap pulled off a coordinated attack all over the country. Everything got hit, and we were not prepared for it.

"Our personnel are mostly ammo specialists, pilots, motor pool, cooks, construction specialists, medical personnel at the hospital, guards at the prison. But of all the personnel, we only have a small reaction force with the 52nd Infantry, and the 576th Ordnance Battalion has its own reaction force of another thirty-two guys. Those guys went outside the perimeter to fight, and part of my job was to coordinate gunship support for them out there.

"The VC blew up tons of ammo here at the depot—we've got to have lost millions of dollars' worth of ammunition. Some of it was started by rockets, and some by VC sappers who had gotten in and placed bombs on the pads of ammunition, and they went off. They think a single 122-millimeter rocket hit one of the pads of ammo—you've seen them—the pads were about half the size of a football field. It started a chain reaction.

"All the unexploded ordnance blew up. We had put berms around each ammo pad, about eight to ten feet high, so that if any pad exploded, the force would go upward to reduce casualties. When the rockets came back down, they hit a pad of flares, and that exploded like fireworks. Then those descended, and started fires all over the depot. There were only eight guys in the depot fire department, but they were leading the way to try to put out all the fires. The rockets and mortars kept coming in from outside the perimeter, and we were getting a ton of sniper fire."

"What about casualties?" I asked.

"There were definitely casualties. Four officers were killed. The VC had a direct hit on the officers' hootch. There would have been a fifth, but the chaplain had left it not thirty seconds before. He was the only one from that hootch who survived."

Bobby paused for a minute. He had known most of the officers.

"I was in the CP, the command post, which was pretty much underground. It was made of thick metal shipping containers about four foot by eight foot, six of them in each row. On top of that, we had a bunker of sandbags over seven feet deep, because supposedly the 122-millimeter rockets could penetrate seven feet. That's why I'm here talking to you."

As if it had just dawned on him, he asked abruptly, "What the heck are you doing back here, anyway?!"

"Well, I went back to Saigon, and I saw a big light up north. I asked an MP what it was, and he said, 'They blew up the Long Binh ammo dump.' I came back to make sure you were okay."

A call came in over the radio:

"Guerrilla through the fence line. Guerrilla through the fence line."

"Holy s—," I said. "Give me a weapon."

"What are you gonna do with it, shoot the monkey?" Bobby asked.

"What?" I was confused. "You mean a sapper dressed in one of those Year of the Monkey costumes?" Nineteen sixty-eight was indeed the Year of the Monkey, which comes around every twelve years.

I searched around the bunker for a gun.

"Here," Bobby offered. "Do you want my survival knife?"

"Sergeant," one of the other soldiers interjected, "I think your friend thinks the guard said *guerrilla*. It's *gorilla*, sir, as in ape!"

"They don't have gorillas in Vietnam!" I said.

"I know that," said Bobby. "But have you ever seen the gibbons or macaques here? And those amazing red-and-yellow-and-blue doucs, too. They're huge. Some of our less sophisticated guys call them all gorillas. We've had a family of 'em in the jungle around the perimeter trying to get in all day. They were probably as freaked out by the explosions as we were. And hungry."

I was still a little nervous. Bobby affected a scared voice.

"Hey, Clyde, you don't think it could be Batutut, do you?"

Clyde paused dramatically. "Could be, Sergeant, could be. There have been sightings!"

I had heard about the tall, red-haired Bigfoot of Vietnam. But they were merely busting my chops.

"Okay, Pappas, now *you* owe *me* a beer!"

The three of us laughed, and we went out again that night. I didn't see a guerrilla, I didn't see an ape. The enlisted men's bar was open, and they let us back in. I was so relieved that Bobby had survived the attack. I would have stayed with him another couple of days, but I had to hurry back to Saigon.

"Okay, Bobby, it's take two, as they say in the movies. I'll see you back in Doc Fiddler's before you can say 'Unique New York' three times fast."

"'New Yeek You Nork,' as we say in Inwood. Thanks for coming back up, Chick. Thanks for giving a damn."

"*Slan abhaile.*"

"Hey, I'm Greek, remember? Don't gimme that Gaelic stuff."

"Okay, safe home. See you soon, buddy." I gave him a big hug and slapped him on the back.

I had to check in at the consulate, or the consular official might think I'd gone missing and be glad of it and throw away my paperwork.

I hitched a ride with some GIs who were headed to Saigon in a jeep. We were driving along the road through the countryside, past fields, mostly. I was daydreaming when out of the tall grasses—*boom!*—came a loud blast and—*whoosh!*—a mortar flew right behind our heads, missing those of us in the backseat by four or five feet. The driver floored it and sped to Saigon. My ears were ringing, but I was glad to still have them, and my head in between.

I was also grateful that Bobby was still alive. I was grateful Tommy Collins was still alive, guarding a POW camp outside Qui Nhon. I was praying that Rick and Kevin and Richie and Joey were okay. I was glad Johnny and the seamen and the folks I'd met in Saigon were okay.

Once I was back there, I stopped into the Notre Dame Basilica to light some candles and say prayers of thanks and hope. The church was so beautiful inside, with its white stucco arches with every brick and tile from France, and stained-glass wildflowers around saints in every window. I felt a bit of peace for the first time in a while. I guess the Buddhist monks were going for the same feeling by burning incense five times a day at their roadside altars.

Meanwhile, Long Binh continued to receive regular rocket and mortar fire, and sniper and machine-gun fire. Bobby survived that, but not everybody did.

CHAPTER 31

HELPING A DESCENDANT OF THE MAYANS

I was worried about my other buddies out there. Each day, the journalists at the Caravelle had been giving us our own private news reports.

According to them, General Earle Gilmore Wheeler, chairman of the Joint Chiefs of Staff, had flown to Vietnam to meet with General Westmoreland. Wheeler said they were considering mobilizing the reserves to invade Laos and Cambodia, and Westmoreland insisted that he would need those 206,000 additional troops for the job. Under Westmoreland's tenure, the number of troops in Vietnam had soared from 16,000 in 1963 to 536,100 by 1968. It would peak at 543,000 early the following year. Wheeler said he'd think about it. He ended up going back to Washington and reporting to LBJ that, despite heavy losses, the North Vietnamese and the Vietcong were not even close to giving up.

Meanwhile, Clark Clifford, an adviser to Presidents Kennedy and Johnson, had taken over as Secretary of Defense after McNamara's exit, and the journos told us that LBJ had asked him to "study the situation." Clifford went "in the tank" with the Joint Chiefs of Staff for three days, asking all kinds of questions, and he didn't like the answers. He went in gung ho and came out wanting to pass the peace pipe with Uncle Ho. Years later, he reflected, "We couldn't win the war . . . and all we were going to do was waste the lives of our men." Clifford denied Westmoreland his gargantuan troop request and convinced LBJ to halve the bombing of North Vietnam, which led to peace talks in 1968. As the top dogs held their debates, I didn't know where all my buddies were as Tet raged on in Hue, Khe Sanh, and elsewhere. But the journos said that we had retaken most of the 120 towns and bases that had been invaded during the Tet offensive.

Try though I might at the US consulate, I still couldn't get the hell out of Dodge, so I decided it might be a good time to try to help Pedro Menchu (not his real name). He was another mariner; I'd found him wandering around Saigon and invited him to join the Caravelle Refugee Roundtable. His country, Guatemala, didn't have an embassy to help him in Vietnam—it was too busy running its own bloody civil war. In his low-key way, he would tell us about the atrocities against the Mayan Indians and the leftists, but then he would encourage us to go see the incredible Mayan ruins in his beautiful homeland.

Ben Hur immediately nicknamed him Mensch for his mellow personality. We couldn't picture it, but he'd organized a strike on board his ship, which his captain called a mutiny. In port, Mensch's own Captain Queeg had handed him over to South Vietnamese police—for a fee. The minute Queeg left the deck, the cops pocketed the dough and told Mensch to scram.

Why feed another man in jail when they didn't have enough food for themselves?

Since then, Mensch hadn't been able to find work anywhere in Saigon. I guess that because he'd been charged with mutiny, he didn't qualify for the union per diem I was getting. He was one of the K'iche' people—the Mayan descendants up in the Guatemalan highlands—and the Vietnamese couldn't make him out. There were plenty of Hispanic American soldiers who fought in Vietnam—170,000, in fact—but, like me, Mensch wasn't in uniform. Maybe the South Vietnamese thought he was Cuban. The Cubans were allies of the North Vietnamese; they had military divisions in Laos all along the Ho Chi Minh Trail. Arizona senator John McCain, a navy pilot who was shot down over North Vietnam and spent six torturous years in captivity, said once that the Cubans were the worst torturers of American POWs at his camp, the notorious Hoa Lo Prison, referred to sardonically as the Hanoi Hilton.

Mensch told me he wanted to join the US Army, as he'd heard it provided a path to American citizenship. They didn't exactly have "Join the Army" signs in Saigon; it would be a bit redundant. I brought Mensch to the Brinks Hotel, looking for a reenlistment officer. Even the officers looked at us as if we were crazy. Who would re-up in the middle of the Tet offensive? It was a little upside down to them. It was like asking for a glass of water while your ship is sinking. But one of them directed us to Tan Son Nhut. So, we headed out to the airfield in the back of a military transport.

When we got there, the South Vietnamese National Police didn't like Mensch's looks either. They squinted at his ID and started to scream at us in Vietnamese. Loosely translated, my guess is they were yelling, *"Get the f— out of the truck!"* There were about twelve of them; some had pistols and some had rifles, and they were all pointing whatever they had right at our heads. Mensch was trembling and looked terrified, which made matters worse.

I said, "Okay! Okay! Calm down! We're leaving!" They kept their guns trained at our heads.

Once we got out, the military transport took off like a shot. The driver definitely did not want to be involved with this BS. I said very matter-of-factly, "Hey, we don't want to make any trouble; we'll come back when you're not so busy." As I did, I waved down another army transport—this one headed back to Saigon—and I asked the young GI driving if we could hitch a ride back. The GI looked at the White Mice, then at Mensch, then at me, right in the eyes, and he "got it" and had the stones to act on it. He gave me a knowing nod.

"Sure," he said casually. "Hop in." The South Vietnamese cops kept their guns pointed at us but let us climb on board, and we took off. God bless that kid.

Once we got back to Saigon, I brought Mensch to the US consulate and asked Heller, the guy who had helped me, to assist him. He said, "I have enough problems with you, Donohue." I left Mensch with him, and he didn't throw him out, so I hope he helped him. For all I know, my Guatemalan acquaintance did join the US Army and rose to the rank of sergeant major.

CHAPTER 32

C.D., PHONE HOME

Major fighting continued in Hue, Khe Sanh, Chu Lai, and other strongholds, but there was one good sign in Saigon. One day I saw that the USO had reopened. The acronym stands for United Service Organizations. The large hall was totally empty; after all, GIs weren't exactly taking R & R in Saigon these days. The brave USO volunteers who'd come from the States to help servicemen and women seemed overjoyed when I walked in; they would have something to do.

I asked if I could use their shortwave radio. In that era before cellphones, that's how soldiers called home: You reached out to ham-radio operators in the States, who would patch collect calls through for servicemen. Ham-radio operators back home were quiet heroes. They worked for hours on their own time in the middle of the night so that young soldiers could hear the voice of their mother or father or their wife or girlfriend for even a few moments for the first time in months. You could close your eyes and feel normal for a while. There was usually a two- or three-hour wait, as all the soldiers in town lined up, but they didn't care.

I hoped they'd let me do it even though I wasn't a service-man. They were glad to. One of the USO volunteers operated the radio, and when he switched it on, that beautiful, scratchy, echoey sound made my heart leap.

"Come in, San Francisco, come in. Saigon USO calling, San Francisco, this is Saigon."

"Hello, Saigon. Brian in San Francisco. The skip is in." *(The weather is allowing for a clear signal.)*

"Can you help us get a collect call to New York?"

"You got it. Be safe. Good luck—and seventy-three." *(Fare-well.)* They pulled out the chair, and I rolled up to the micro-phone. The time difference was eleven hours, so it was four o'clock in the morning in New York. You know, the time of night when if the phone rings, you bolt upright in bed and blurt out, "Who's dead?!"

"Hello?" I heard my father's voice in the echo; groggy sounding, with a nervous edge to it.

"Hello, Dad."

A few seconds of silence passed.

"Chickie?!!!!! Where the hell are you?!"

"I'm in Saigon."

"Saigon! That's what the Colonel told me, but I didn't be-lieve it! You're not supposed to be in Vietnam! Everyone has been looking for you!"

And, then, the clincher:

"Do you know what you're doing to your mother?!"

I will never forget that. It was as if I were a teenager again, calling him late from Rockaway Beach. I heard my father speak to my mother for a minute, and then he put her on the phone. She was the typical loving mother.

"Are you all right, Chickie?"

"I'm okay, Mom."

"Are you getting enough to eat?"

"Yeah, Mom, I'm getting plenty to eat."

I paused. I was trying not to get choked up. She hadn't heard from me in three months, yet there wasn't one word of reproach. For my father, the reproach was his form of concern. I hadn't really taken into consideration how I would worry them should they find out, and with half the old neighborhood knowing my whereabouts, of course they did.

"Chickie?"

"Yes, Ma."

"When are you going to come home?"

"Soon, Ma. Soon."

A merchant marine Great White Fleet ship like the
SS Limon, *from which I was able to get food and
supplies for the Caravelle bar.*

CHAPTER 33

PLEASE *DO* FEED
THE ANIMALS

The marines weren't taking volunteers, and Heller still wouldn't let me on one of the big C-130 Hercules planes that transported soldiers, airmen, and sailors, living or dead, back to the States.

The French agent was still at his country house; he wasn't about to come back until Tet was over. So, I dealt with Mr. Minh. We spoke about his family, his friends. He was highly educated. Like Ho Chi Minh, he had been sent to boarding school in France. But he had been of service to the French and to the Americans, and that would surely seal his doom if the North Vietnamese succeeded in taking over.

Yet despite his troubles, and though for the first time he seemed a little hunched over, Mr. Minh wasn't worried about himself. He was worried about something else, and that was clear when I showed up one day with a small parcel of groceries for him.

"Please," Mr. Minh said, "bring it to the zoo."

"The zoo?!" I asked, incredulous.

The night Tet began, large numbers of Vietcong guerrillas had lain in wait in the city's cemeteries, parks, the racetrack, and, Mr. Minh said, the Saigon Zoo. They had emerged from their hiding places, including a seventy-five-mile multilevel network of underground tunnels, like the catacombs, under the Cu Chi district of the capital city. That's where the Vietcong stored ammo, weapons, food, medicine, and radio equipment, and hid for days with little air, plagued by rats and scorpions. Australian and American soldiers—nicknamed tunnel rats—who descended into this hell, armed only with pistols, flashlights, and string, were met with punji sticks or booby traps or waiting VC.

According to Mr. Minh, some of the Vietcong had crawled out of the tunnels the first night of Tet and into the zoo, an ideal spot from which to launch an offensive. It had fifty acres of botanical gardens right off the river and nobody watching but the monkeys. The VC had killed the zookeepers first thing, and the animals had remained locked up and abandoned ever since.

Some Saigon residents had gone in there and found the starving animals. These people were hungry themselves, yet they brought whatever they could spare. Maybe they were like Mr. Minh, a devout Buddhist who believed in reincarnation. He really didn't see much difference between the animals and us.

"The Buddha told us that an animal might be your ancestor," Mr. Minh explained. "Perhaps they did things in life that made them come back as an elephant. Though animals live in a different realm, they feel as we do. They have potential for enlightenment. And if they do achieve it, when they die, they may come back in the next life as human again. We must help them."

If Mr. Minh felt so strongly about it, I was determined to check it out, though I still had human mouths to feed. I discreetly tucked the nonperishable groceries inside a jardinière in his garden to give him the next day and headed straight to the zoo, buying bags of peanuts from street vendors along the way. I reached the zoo's elaborate wrought iron gate, built by the French a hundred years before. It was wide open.

There was a garden full of dead orchids. An ungodly screeching came from the canopy; I looked up, and hundreds of green parrots hung upside down from the trees. Ahead, elephants with sagging skin stood listlessly in the heat. White tigers and leopards paced in their cages; monkeys scrambled frantically in theirs. I saw an old lady feed a baguette to a crocodile through some iron bars. Man, did he snap it up, practically taking off her hand. Another lady was pushing small bowls of rice into the monkey cage. I don't know if monkeys usually eat rice, but they were going crazy for it now.

The Vietnamese government didn't have food for its people, let alone zoo animals. These folks were probably giving half of what little they had to the beasts. The same thing happened in Berlin and Budapest after World War II. Kindness shows up in surprising places.

I went straight to see John on the *Limon*, and this time I took not one but two big duffel bags with me. I was going to give the gang at the Caravelle a feast, and I was going to give the beasts a feast, too. When I told the seamen the story, they were outraged. They went through the freezer, asking questions such as: "Do monkeys eat spare ribs?" "What about corn on the cob? They must like it; they're like us."

"Speak for yourself," said another.

By the time I left, night had fallen. I could barely walk down the gangway with my two Santa bags, and I knew I couldn't carry them all the way to the zoo, my first stop.

Down at the dock, I set the bags on the street and hailed a guy on a big motorcycle. He had no problem with the bags; they carry anything on those bikes: fighting cocks in cages, three kids, grandma. He set the bags in front of him, I hopped on the back, and he tore off. I wondered why he was speeding down traffic-jammed Tu Do Street so fast, and my questions were answered when shots rang out. The motorcyclist was hit, and we hit the ground hard, sliding along the street until we came to a stop with the bike on top of us.

He was ripped to shreds on his left side, his leg torn open to the bone. His shirt was stained with blood from bullet wounds. My hands and face were scraped up, and blood was dripping, but I was a lot better off than he was.

A few minutes passed, and we lay there like sitting ducks. I was a little out of it but worried the sniper would go after us again. People helped pull us to the sidewalk. A siren blared louder and louder, and up came an open-air ambulance, like a jeep ambulance, with red flags bearing white crosses—the flag of Switzerland, where the Red Cross was also born. Two Swiss EMT volunteers ran out, loaded the biker onto a stretcher and into the ambulance. When they came back for me, I said, "No, no, I'll be all right. Take care of him." They said in German accents that they were going to the Seventeenth Field Hospital, which had been retaken.

They gave me a bottle of peroxide and bandages and sped off. I looked in the street and the smashed-up bike had vanished. So had one of the duffel bags—I found the other, but it had been completely torn open and ransacked, with frozen peas spilling out of it all over the street. Maybe that was the point of the shooting in the first place: robbery, not politics. I was just glad I could walk away from it all.

I limped back to the Frenchman's house. The Caravelle and the zoo would have to wait. Mr. Minh answered the door, and he jumped back in fear for a minute till I said, "It's me, John Donohue." My face was covered in blood, and I guess I looked like hell. He peered out the door in both directions and then pulled me inside by the elbow.

I had never been past the front office before, but this time he took me to the bathroom in the back of the house. I was shocked by the opulence, especially considering the poverty out in the street. Carved mahogany furniture, oil paintings, gilt-framed mirrors, silk curtains, Oriental carpets. Like a socialite's Fifth Avenue apartment. It probably belonged to the shipping agency and had been passed down since the French colonial days.

Mr. Minh helped me wash up at the bathroom sink, which had gold faucets. Two toilets were side by side. I asked him what the hell was that about—togetherness for a husband and wife? He burst out laughing, despite the circumstances. "One is a bidet, for woman or man," Mr. Minh explained. "You never saw a bidet?" No, I hadn't. We didn't have bidets in Inwood.

I cleaned up as well as I could. I had a couple bad scrapes, and he applied Mercurochrome antiseptic and bandaged my leg and my arm. My clothes were torn up, but I'd live. "Please follow me," he said in his soothing voice. He led me through hallways lined from floor to ceiling with books and into a kitchen that was bigger than some apartments I've had in New

York. "Would you like some soup?" he asked. Provisions were still hard to get, and that's probably all he had. I would tell him to peek in the jardinière when I left.

"No, no thanks, I'm not hungry," I said. "A beer would be nice, if you've got one."

He did: a French Bière de Noël probably left over from Christmas, and full of clove and cinnamon. But he also had a Belgian St. Feuillien. The label said it was named after an Irish monk named Foillan. Brother Foillan had come through a forest there in Belgium in the seventh century to preach the Gospel. Unfortunately, the folks living there at the time didn't appreciate his message, and they decapitated him. I thought it was nice that a Belgian brewery would remember a fellow Irishman in this way, so I chose the St. Feuillien. I sipped it as we sat at the table.

Minh looked at me. "You're going to leave us," he said sadly.

"I've been trying to leave here since day one, Mr. Minh, you know that."

"No, I mean all of you. All of you Americans. The French abandoned us, and now you will, too. When will my poor country ever have peace? You know, our Shakespeare, Nguyen Du, wrote metaphorically that we are 'rich in beauty, unlucky in life . . . How many harrowing events have occurred while mulberries cover the conquered sea?'"

I don't think old Mr. Minh was afraid, even though he would surely be a goner if the North Vietnamese took over. He had collaborated with the French and the major American suppliers of the war. I think he had a dream in his youth of seeing his country become a free democracy before he passed on to the next incarnation. I could tell, though, that his optimism had taken a hit since Tet.

"Mr. Minh, look at that beautiful Saigon Bridge. We built that, and we built the highway leading to it, and the other bridges leading to that, and we built the airport at the other end. Do you really think that after the US government spent millions of American taxpayer dollars building a whole infrastructure of highways and bridges and airports and buildings all over your country that we would leave it all behind for Ho Chi Minh to grab?"

I said it to cheer him up, but I wasn't sure I believed it. And I wanted to go home, I wanted my friends serving there to go home, and I wanted all the mariners and all the soldiers in Vietnam to go home. Ben Hur and Mensch and the Aussies and the ROKs and all the journalists—I wanted them all to arrive home safe, unless, of course, they wanted to stay. *Slan abhaile,* as we say in Gaelic. Safe journey home.

CHAPTER 34

"WE CANNOT WIN"

In the accident, I'd lost all the food I would ordinarily bring to the Caravelle. I didn't look so good, either, so I skipped the socializing and headed back to my humble abode. The next day, I tried again, taking two bags of food and making deliveries to Mr. Minh's, the folks at Nuong's hotel, the animals at the zoo, and, finally, the Caravelle rooftop. No ambushes this time, thankfully.

The reporters, when you saw them, had their hands full with all the breaking stories they had to cover. They were charged up; this is what they were born to do, and some of them risked their lives doing it. And what they were seeing was not pretty: February had started with the chief of the National Police, General Nguyen Ngoc Loan, shooting Vietcong prisoner Nguyen Van Lem point-blank in the head on a Saigon street as cameras rolled. NBC cameraman Vo Suu caught it on film, and Associated Press photographer Eddie Adams snapped the shot seen 'round the world, turning more Americans against the war and winning Adams a Pulitzer Prize.

CBS anchor Walter Cronkite, the nation's most respected newsman, who had himself been a courageous foreign correspondent in World War II, decided to fly to Vietnam in mid-February and witness Tet for himself. He reunited with his old acquaintance General Creighton Abrams, whom he'd first met in World War II. Abrams is said to have told Cronkite, "We cannot win this goddamn war, and we ought to find a dignified way out."

Cronkite went on the air on the evening of February 27, 1968, and said, "It is increasingly clear to this reporter that the only rational way out, then, will be to negotiate, not as victors, but as an honorable people who lived up to their pledge to defend democracy and did the best they could." Then presidential aide Bill Moyers was with Lyndon Johnson as he watched Cronkite's editorial. LBJ lamented to him, "If I've lost Cronkite, I've lost Middle America." A month later, the president would announce that he would not seek reelection in the fall.

Meanwhile, the Tet offensive continued for weeks in Saigon's outskirts, as well as in the imperial city, Hue, in Khe Sanh, and other towns and military sites. From February 11 to February 17 alone, 543 Americans were killed and 2,547 were wounded, making it the deadliest week of the entire war. Five days later, the US Selective Service System announced a new draft call for 48,000 more boys to add to the half million already in Vietnam.

On February 29, leap year day, appropriately, McNamara officially walked away from the war he'd helped escalate. He and LBJ, himself about to back out of the war without ending it, got stuck in a Pentagon elevator for twelve minutes on their way to McNamara's retirement ceremony. There was something symbolic about that. They got out, but all 536,100 boys were still stuck.

In my own way, I was stuck, too. Soon it was March, and gaining on Saint Patrick's Day. There isn't any parade in Saigon on Saint Patrick's, and I never like to miss the parade. It looked like I wasn't leaving anytime soon.

During the Tet offensive, Bobby Pappas's base at Long Binh suffered major sapper explosions; Kevin McLoone was sent with the Americal Division to Chu Lai, where they were rocketed and mortared for a month; Tommy Collins fought the Viet Cong in Qui Nhon; and Rick Duggan (pictured) was sent to Quang Tri City, the A Shau Valley, and Khe Sanh.

CHAPTER 35

"WE'RE OUTTA HERE!"

The Vietcong knew that the ships in the river were sitting ducks, and one night, they went hunting. They rocketed the SS *Limon*, with Johnny Jackson and the other seamen on it; and they hit another ship, the SS *US Tourist*, downriver. The *Tourist* had supposedly anchored in a safer place: a tributary of the Saigon River down south near Cat Lai. All the VC needed was a Russian shoulder-fired RPG-7 rocket launcher to strike it from the riverbank. Or they could have snuck past the South Vietnamese cops in a truck with a Russian A-19 field cannon inside, which could shoot howitzer shells five inches wide up to six miles away.

Whichever they used, nine shells hit the *Tourist*, and though seamen suffered minor injuries, all nine missed the big target: the ship's cargo was ammunition, and had it ignited, it would have been Long Binh all over again.

When the *Limon* was hit, some of the seamen were wounded. I was so thankful that Johnny was okay and that nobody had been killed. The captain was heard yelling, "That's it! We're getting the hell out of here!" Merchant ship captains were contracted to the US military, but they had (arguably) more autonomy aboard their ships than even navy admirals had. Admirals are part of a larger system, but merchant captains hold the title master of the vessel. At sea, the captain of a commercial ship has absolute power, and John and the other seamen sure appreciated that at the moment.

The *Limon*'s captain called the US Coast Guard—probably the commander who'd tried to help me—and reportedly told him that he didn't care if he used scab longshoremen, the US Army, or his grandmother. "If this ship isn't unloaded in the next three days," he said, "I'm bringing all this food to Manila." There were still plenty of comestibles left, even after Johnny's and his shipmates' generous donations to Saigon.

The next morning, a chain of about a hundred longshore-men decided it might be a good idea to end their strike or lose their jobs. They were unloading the ship under heavy US MP guard. They were the skinniest longshoremen I'd ever seen. I hoped some of the food would "fall off the truck" in their direction.

The captain got word on the morning they were to set sail that they were an oiler short. One of the crew members injured in the attack was still in the hospital and couldn't be moved. I was sorry for the guy, hurt and stuck, but by the grace of God, I took it as a sign. I rushed over to the *Limon*. I was an oiler, and I was a union rep, so I knew the union rules: if a qualified union crew member in the port was looking for work, the ship could not sail "short." John took me to the captain, and I asked for the oiler job. The captain turned me down and said he was going to have the guys double up and take on overtime shifts, but John showed him the union rule book. He looked it over with furrowed brow as I bit my lip, and finally, he said, "What the hell, be back on board by 0800 hours.

"The SS *Limon* waits for no man now," he added, kind of profoundly.

It was 1900 now—thirteen hours away.

"Don't be late," warned John.

I was about to hurry off the ship, but on deck I stopped and thought about it: I didn't have any possessions to pack. I was paid up at the hotel. There were guys in Saigon I wanted to say good-bye to: Ben Hur, the Aussies, the journos, and the others at the Caravelle; Nuong, the young cop; and Mr. Minh, the shipping clerk. I would even go back and thank Heller at the embassy if I had time. They had all sustained me in different ways.

I couldn't say good-bye to Dao—Peach Blossom. I had said to her that when things settled down, we could sail over to Phu Quoc Island, where Captain Kidd's treasure is supposedly buried. I said I'd buy her a puppy: one of those rare blue-tongued Vietnamese ridgebacks with webbed feet that can hunt and swim and climb trees and catch a scent a mile away.

Most of all, I wished I could check back with Tommy Collins and Rick Duggan and Kevin McLoone and Bobby Pappas and all their pals and fellow soldiers. I wished I could have found more guys on my list. I worried about them all. But I couldn't chance even going into town in case the captain decided to leave immediately. Or if somebody decided to pick me off or detain me for fun. I was onboard now, and I wasn't about to disembark before we got to the States. I found a quiet place on deck and wished them all well and prayed that they would be all right.

At 0800 hours, we set sail. I watched Saigon fade into the distance, and then I set to work on the engine. Before long, we were out in the ocean, on the way home to the good old USA.

CHAPTER 36

I KISS THE GROUND

We stopped in Subic Bay, the Philippines, to fuel up, but from then on, we sailed across the Pacific. I was never so happy to be below deck in a hot engine room.

After about three weeks, we landed in Seattle. I think I was the first one down the gangplank, and I literally kissed the ground of the United States.

I got my pay, nearly $2,000; Johnny got his, plus he received a "vessel attack bonus" for being on the ship when the rockets hit. My friend planned to stay with the *Limon*, which was probably going back to Vietnam. Not me. I was headed to New York, so we parted ways. Johnny reached out his hand, and I grabbed him and gave him a big hug. The guy had kept me and a lot of other people—and animals—alive during the entire Tet offensive.

I headed straight downtown for the first department store I could find, which turned out to be a J. C. Penney. There I bought underwear, socks, a pair of pants, and a shirt. I also picked up a pair of shoes—even a jacket. I asked them to clip the tags off everything, and I walked into the fitting room, put

on the new clothes, and threw my old ones—the jeans and madras shirt that I had basically been wearing for four months—
into a garbage can.

I hiked to the nearest big hotel and saw a line of cabs waiting
out front. I asked the first driver to take me to the airport.

"What airline?" he said.

"Any airline that flies to New York," I said.

He took me to American Airlines, and I bought a ticket in
coach. For some reason—maybe because the plane was two-
thirds empty—they bumped me up to first class.

A middle-aged guy in a suit was sitting next to me. He asked
me where I was headed, and I just said, "Home."

I guess that, despite my fresh new outfit, I looked a little
worse for wear, or maybe because I was young, he asked me
if I was coming back from 'Nam. I told him yeah, but that I
hadn't served, I had been . . . visiting a few friends. "It's a long
story," I said.

He replied, "We have about six hours on this flight, and I'm
all ears. How about a drink?"

He was drinking one of those cocktails they serve on planes,
and I said, "Whatever you're drinking, I'm drinking." Appropriately enough, it was a Manhattan. I'd never had one before
or since, but I had about four of them while I told him my
story. Then, at some point, out the window, the skyscrapers
of New York City appeared, and I teared up. They looked like
they were fist-pumping the sky. I couldn't wait to leave the
plane at JFK Airport.

I thanked the businessman, went out and hailed a taxi, and
told the driver to head straight to Inwood, Manhattan. More
specifically: "To Doc Fiddler's Bar on Sherman Avenue and

Isham Street." It was nighttime, and the city looked even bigger and sparklier than when I left—as if crystals had shot up out of the East River. I was lucky to be coming home, when others hadn't. I hoped my buddies would come home soon, too.

I had gone to show them a gesture of support. I guess you could call it an extreme gesture of support. As the taxi wended its way to Inwood, I was thinking about whether what I had done was as totally reckless and crazy as some had said to me. Then the cab pulled up in front of Doc Fiddler's— where it all began.

I walked in, and the bar was nearly full. Somebody spotted me and yelled out:

"Colonel! It's Chickie!!"

Georgie Lynch, aka the Colonel—whose idea this journey was—yelled out, "Holy s—, Chick, you're alive!"

"Yeah, I'm alive, and so are Tommy and Rick and Kevin and Bobby."

There was pandemonium, and I didn't care anymore whether it had been a reckless thing to do. The Colonel, who never drank on duty, poured himself and everyone else a beer and raised it:

"To Chickie," he said, "who brought our boys beer, respect, pride—and love, goddamn it!"

There were cheers and more toasts and more storytelling. I saw they had a map over the bar on which they had been trying to trace my journey from Rick's report and letters from the guys. Much later, somebody offered to drive me home, so I asked him to take me to my parents' house in New Jersey. It was in the wee hours by now, and I rang the bell awhile until my father finally answered. When he opened the door and saw me, he called out, "Oh my God! Catherine, it's Chickie!"

My mother came running out in her robe, and she hugged me tight and cried for a while. She said, "Chickie, promise me you'll never go back to Vietnam again."

I said, "Oh, I promise, Ma. I promise."

That was an easy promise to keep.

REFLECTIONS ON THE JOURNEY

When I returned to New York, I didn't see Vietnam the same way. I thought of the twenty-year-old kids dead and their families destroyed, all because of egos and miscalculations at the top. I had a lot on my mind, and it took a long while to sort out my feelings.

I resumed my life as a merchant mariner, although I remained on the beach for a couple of months before putting out to sea again. I sailed on a coastwise tanker, back and forth from the Gulf Coast to New England. Since the ship didn't travel to a foreign port, I was not obligated to sign a contract, which allowed me to quit at any time. I did just that one day in New Orleans. I tried to figure things out in New Orleans, but, as much as I loved that town, it was airing the same nightly news broadcasts as in New York, dominated by coverage of the war and the protests against it.

Demonstrations against the war or the draft were erupting on campus after campus across the country. These reports disturbed me, and when I searched for news of the troops in Vietnam, I usually found the soldiers' combat stories buried deep in the pages of the newspapers or late in the TV news. The media rarely seemed to show how patriotic our troops were or how low their morale was, though they did report on the high rate of drug use among them.

What they gave was body counts. They'd present the number of casualties suffered on both sides like it was a football score: "Enemy dead, 346; US casualties, 'only' 25." It was as if we were winning a game, not sacrificing the lives of our young soldiers—or theirs. GIs' obits would be little more than blurbs in the paper. If you were lucky, they would provide a name, age, and the high school from which he had recently graduated. Was he an only child? A budding scientist? A future baseball star? A young father? Was he the one who made his squad laugh in grim moments? They died before they'd even begun to live. It's not as if the public forgot them; Americans never found out enough about the boys to remember them.

Even now, so many of the 58,307 names (including those of 8 women) on the Vietnam Veterans Memorial Fund's Wall of Faces website don't have stories to go with them. It was left to family and friends to keep the votive candles burning.

It begged the question "Was it worth it?" That question gnawed at me and was affecting my very identity. I decided to travel to County Cork, Ireland, where my grandmother Abina Donohue had grown up before she immigrated to America at the end of the eighteen hundreds. Something about those rolling green farmlands in County Cork gave me peace and enabled me to see the whole world—the world beyond my neighborhood. Coverage of our war and our protests didn't dominate the news on their "telly."

What did dominate their news was Ireland's Troubles. It was ironic to be in Ireland at this time. I realized my relatives were in a similar situation to the Vietnamese. In Vietnam, a large percentage of the population was determined to expel the last of the foreign armies that had occupied their land off and on since 111 BC. The Chinese, the French, and the Japanese during World War II—when Ho Chi Minh and his Viet Minh independence forces helped us in our war against Japan, only to have us agree to hand back Vietnam to the French after VJ Day—and now we Americans had all taken turns ruling that slip of a country.

The Irish were occupied for nine hundred years, but only by the English, who took away the Irish people's lands, their right to practice their religion, their right to vote. They let their children starve during the Great Famine, and now, in the late 1960s, the sectarian violence and political fighting in Northern Ireland was heating up. My relatives talked of little else. It was hard not to do a compare and contrast in my mind, to wonder, What's the difference?

The difference, of course, is that the Irish were not Communists. But now, half the clothes I see in stores have "Made in Vietnam" tags on them. We do business with China; hell, we borrow money from Chinese billionaires. We've loosened our embargo a bit in Cuba. With Laos and North Korea, those are the last five countries on the planet to still call themselves Communist, but other than North Korea, they barely qualify. Don't they all come around to a market economy eventually? Many of them peacefully?

I was spurred to go to Vietnam by the sight of antiwar demonstrators in Central Park protesting against my friends from the neighborhood who were serving in the military. Having served overseas in the marines myself, I could only imagine what my buddies were feeling as they heard what was going on in letters from home or from new recruits. Meanwhile, they were facing down terror and being harassed when they returned home.

I had felt that what the protesters were doing was un-American. In fact, I felt they were traitors. I felt that they were taking advantage of our American rights, without paying for those rights. What other country would allow its citizens to protest against its own army in the field, waving our enemy's flag? They were calling our own loyal citizens murderers, while those members of the armed services were endangering their lives—sacrificing their lives—in defense of our allies, just as our fathers and uncles had done twenty-five years earlier in World War II. I felt they were stabbing our own in the back.

While I was in Vietnam, what I was seeing did not jibe with the official reports out of our military command or out of Washington. After I stood outside the US embassy as a very few heroic boys fought and died to take it back, and General Westmoreland held a presser after it was safe to come out, making his statement about "the enemy's well-laid plans" going "afoul," it made me question the official line.

If the plans were well laid and Westmoreland knew about them, which he did, and he knew that five cities had been attacked twenty-four hours before Tet launched, why didn't he have more than four marines and two army MPs guarding our embassy and consulate compound in Saigon? Or his own headquarters at Tan Son Nhut Air Base, where MPs were overwhelmed by a VC battalion? Why weren't more combat-ready troops armed and on real alert in the 120 cities and bases when the offensive launched in earnest? With half the South Vietnamese army on vacation for the holiday truce? On that moonless night, 246 American boys would die, the deadliest day in the war.

Westmoreland kept asking for more and more boys to be sent over, when South Vietnamese President Thieu didn't even have a draft for South Vietnam's own eighteen- and nineteen-year-olds, like we did, and the South Vietnamese did almost nothing to draft evaders, especially rich ones. My friend Bobby Pappas was drafted away from his wife and baby, only to see four of his officers killed together in the same hootch. Tommy Collins, who lost his friend, another MP, during Tet, suffered severe exposure to Agent Orange, the toxic defoliant containing dioxin that the US dropped on the jungles to strip away the enemy's coverage and food supply. Kevin McLoone was rocketed and mortared for days in hellish Chu Lai with the Americal Division, south of Da Nang. And Ricky Duggan, who landed in Vietnam at age nineteen on the Fourth of July, would engage in 153 combat assaults, including a firefight in the Central Highlands that lasted six days after an entire North Vietnamese regiment surrounded them, armed with Russian and Chinese machine guns that shot a thousand rounds per minute. During Tet, Rick was sent to the haunted A Shau Valley and to Khe Sanh, LBJ's and Westmoreland's obsession.

Westmoreland wanted more boys like Inwood's Tommy Minogue, who died throwing his body over his commander and the platoon's only radio operator so he could call for help that would save the rest of the platoon. Tommy wouldn't make twenty-one.

Gradually, I began to see that the protesters, however disrespectfully, were at least trying to stop this madness. They weren't acknowledging that so many young men were doing what they truly believed was their duty—to their country, their family, their neighborhood. They weren't acknowledging that the soldiers were patriots, that they were heroes. We, in turn, didn't see at the time that the protesters loved our country, too. What they didn't like was our leadership. They were trying to stop more boys from being killed for somebody else's legacy. After what I'd witnessed on my journey, I could definitely agree with that.

If there is one thing that I learned as a result of my Vietnam experience it's that government—all governments for that matter—are not to be trusted. Many politicians lie when it serves their interests. That knowledge served me well in the work I went into, representing the Sandhogs Union, construction trades, and other union workers, and trying to secure support for jobs and legislation from elected officials in New York City, New York State, and Washington, DC. I can't bring back the boys who died, but I can help their brothers and sisters. I hope I've done a little bit of good.

John "Chick" Donohue

WHERE ARE THEY NOW?

During the war, soldiers had darkly funny sayings engraved on their Zippo lighters or markered on their helmets. "When I die, I'm going straight to Heaven," read one motto, "because I've already been to Vietnam."

After Chick bid farewell to each of his buddies in Vietnam, they entered another ring of Hell as the Tet offensive raged on. He had no idea where or how they were until he—or they—returned home.

He had Richard (Richie) Reynolds Jr. on his list, but he never found him, because the young Marine Second Lieutenant was killed the day after Chick arrived. Reynolds's younger brother Kevin said that the twenty-three-year-old officer was leading his platoon, part of the Third Marine Division's A Company, in a charge to rescue a scouting party near Dong Ha, the northernmost town of Vietnam, that was surrounded by more than three hundred North Vietnamese Army regulars. Reynolds was machine-gunned down from atop his amphibious troop carrier, killed along with twelve of his men, but the scouting party was saved.

Chick also didn't find Joey McFadden, but for a less tragic reason. Joey had been sent home, as were all soldiers who contracted malaria twice in the monsoon-soaked, mosquito-infected jungle. His brother Steve (Pally) McFadden said that Joey arrived home in the middle of the night and didn't want to wake their mother and sister. "We quietly went into our room," Pally recalled, "and he told me everything he had seen. He talked for hours. Then he never spoke of the war again." The two brothers would later open McFadden's Saloon, which Nora Ephron would use as the setting for her Broadway play *Lucky Guy,* starring Tom Hanks.

"The Tet offensive started just days after I met Chick; and everything got churned up," recalled Kevin McLoone, the Marine who'd returned to Vietnam as a civilian to help make helicopters safer. "Chick must have had trouble getting around because everything was shut down. Everything was off limits for about a month, especially the military installations.

"The whole country got hit. We were in the bunker and about fifteen to twenty mortar rounds came in. I started second-guessing myself: What the hell am I doing back here in Vietnam? The guy I'd flown up with turned around and went home the next day. I don't blame him—he probably thought he'd be working in a hangar.

"Everybody was moving. The Cav [First Air Cavalry] moved east and north. We moved to Chu Lai, and hooked up with the Army's Americal Division at the air base there. It was quite a show there for about a month. It was pretty nasty. We worked on all their helicopters and planes.

"At Chu Lai, we got rocketed and mortared every few days for a while during Tet. You can live with the mortars. The mortars they used were 60 millimeter and 81 millimeter. The bigger ones can mess you up. The small ones, they'd have to get pretty close to do damage.

"It's the rockets that scare you. Even if you're in the bunker, the rockets you feel. And they scream when they come in. They make this weird noise. We lost guys, for sure.

"In Chu Lai there were C-130s, F4 planes, and A-4D fighter planes—the Skyhawks—single-seat bombers that McDonnell Douglas built for the Marine Corps that could fly up to 670 mph and carry the same weight of munitions as B-17s could during World War II. They also had a lot of helicopters—all Hueys. They were all sitting targets.

"So Chu Lai was on lockdown—you couldn't go anywhere," he continues. "And near Chu Lai, there are absolutely beautiful beaches. That whole area—China Beach, Hoi An, Da Nang—it's beautiful up there. After Tet, we went swimming there.

"Later, they sent us to Nha Trang and Phu Hiep to scramble the aircraft radios there, and to Red Beach in Da Nang. Tet was the most violent couple of months of the whole war. We lost a lot of people. During Tet, we were inflicting more casualties on them than they were on us, but it didn't matter. We were winning numbers-wise but, still, we were losing too many people. My cousin died. All kinds of people we knew died.

"And we got the bad publicity. Nobody back in the States had known how the war was really going. Westmoreland had been giving them stories, but the cameras showed reality."

By 1969, McLoone says he and his colleagues at Dynalectron had scrambled the radio signals "of just about every Huey in country," and after two years, it was time to go home. "My sister was getting married, and she said she would never forgive me if I didn't give her away."

McLoone went on to work for Westinghouse and Fuji Tech, and to marry Margo, whom, he says, "I've known my whole life" and with whom he has two grandchildren, Carly and Alexis. McLoone reconnected with Chick as soon as he returned home to Long Beach, New York. The two diehard Giants fans would attend every game, even away games, by renting a Winnebago and driving to far-flung stadiums. At least on these roads they knew they wouldn't be attacked, unless it was by opposing fans. A voracious reader, McLoone has stayed in shape by playing tennis, riding bikes, and enjoying the snowbird life with his wife in Jupiter, Florida.

Tommy Collins, the young MP Chick first found in Qui Nhon, says that when he came home, "They didn't give you any orientation on what to expect. We arrived at the airport and they were screaming 'Babykillers!' at us. When I got back to the neighborhood, a car backfired and I hit the dirt. I didn't know what the hell was going on for a while."

Collins took the test for the New York City Police Department and he remembers the day he was called: June 30, 1969, to the 32nd precinct in Harlem. The seventies were a rough time and the 32nd a tough place: twenty-two cops in Collins's precinct were shot or stabbed, and five were killed, including partners Waverly Jones, who was African American, and Joe Piagentini, who was shot thirteen times, both from behind, by members of the Black Liberation Army. Perhaps it was Inwood street sense, or his Vietnam military police experience, but Collins earned his gold shield within three years. "You know just about enough not to get yourself into trouble," Collins quips. He was given the job of training five new recruits, part of the NYC Police Academy's first class of women allowed to work the street, including beautiful Suzanne Oquendo. The two have been happily married for twenty-nine years.

After aiding the Narcotics Task Force, Collins was one of the detectives asked to form the new Career Criminal Unit, focusing on perps who had been convicted of murder, armed robbery, or other serious crimes. Collins worked on the infamous "Tuxedo King" case, where kidnappers kept a wealthy garment manufacturer buried alive for twelve days. "I loved the job," Collins says. "I'd still do it if I could." Collins and Suzanne have retired, but they haven't stopped working. Snowbirds in Ft. Myers, Florida, Tommy works at the spring training camp of the Minnesota Twins, and Suzanne works for the Boston Red Sox; they try not to argue about their beloved baseball.

Meanwhile, after Chick left Rick Duggan near the DMZ, his company engaged in some of the fiercest fighting of the Tet offensive. Rick engaged in 153 combat assaults in his time in Vietnam and was awarded the Purple Heart after being wounded in a six-day battle. Many other awards came later. Best of all, he is armed with a chiseled wit about life.

The First US Cavalry Division was sent closer to Quang Tri City at Landing Zone Sharon soon after Chick left Rick. They were ordered to block approaches to the city, as well as attack a base that the North Vietnamese built in the hills about ten miles to the west. An entire North Vietnamese Army battalion invaded the city, and it was one of the key battles of Tet. It lasted from 2 a.m. New Year's until noon the day after; but they were chasing NVA soldiers out of there for about ten days.

Duggan recalls, "We went up to LZ Sharon to secure the perimeter. We had success in cutting off their supplies. They [army strategists] relocated us again after that into the low-lands, and we got into a firefight near the coast that lasted a day or two."

It was then that Duggan was called home. "We were in the field when I was suddenly notified that my father was on his deathbed," recalls Duggan. "I was to leave immediately to say good-bye to him. The military supposedly did this for every-one, but especially when the Red Cross got involved, which they did.

"They whisked me out like nobody's business to Cam Ranh Bay. Twelve hours later, I was on a plane with six coffins and two other guys headed to Okinawa and then Alaska. We landed in Alaska in a blizzard, and the two other guys and I were still in our camo uniforms and we were freezing as the plane refu-eled. We took off for Dover Air Force Base in Delaware, and I took a bus up to New York from there, where my brothers met me at Port Authority. Thank God they brought me a coat.

"We went directly to the hospital, and I was absolutely filthy still from the field. I went into a rest room and literally had to scrape the dirt from my neck and arms before I saw my father.

"My father lived. I thought, maybe since I had done most of my tour, they'll let me stay. But no go. At least, back in the neighborhood that night, I was able to stop into Doc Fiddler's and tell the Colonel that Chick had found me, and that he had found Tommy and Kevin, so far. A roar went up in the bar.

"But since my father didn't die, the army told me I had to go back immediately, to fly out to the Oakland Army Termi-nal in California and, from there, fly back to Vietnam. I flew right out to California and got to the base and caught a flight on a C-141, the huge cargo plane with canvas seats on the sides. I was back in Vietnam in twenty-seven hours, and then right onto a supply chopper to An Khe. I was back in the field within five hours of arrival in Vietnam. The guys were glad to see me—they thought I was dead. Later, we were sent to Khe Sanh toward the end of the siege there. The marines took a beating there, they really did.

"Then we were sent to the A Shau Valley, which was the most bizarre place I have ever been in my life. It was where 17 Green Berets, 200 South Vietnamese Irregulars, and a MIKE Force [Mobile Strike Force Command] company of Montagnards had gotten attacked by four battalions of the North Vietnamese Army in '66. Later, when Tet started, the NVA had gotten a battalion in there and we had done an air assault and we prepped it with artillery and took them by surprise. It was a key locale for them, so close to the Ho Chi Minh Trail in Laos.

"We got there in a mist, and it looked really strange, like Jurassic Park. Huge craters where the artillery shells had landed. There were no villages, no hootches. The NVA had abandoned trucks loaded with mortars and other trucks stacked with Chinese and Russian rifles—we seized all that. We recovered ammo they had stockpiled. All the guys from rural areas back home took souvenir rifles. I didn't want one. Nobody from New York wanted a rifle.

"We patrolled different areas, every day a different event, maybe night operations, go support this unit, go support somebody else. Being a grunt, a foot soldier, a rifleman, it's the old, 'Yours is not to reason why.' You don't know what's going on at the Command Center, what they're planning, what their strategy is. You're told what the objective is, and hopefully you're successful. That's the deal.

"It did get a little sketchy toward the end for us, because the NVA guys that we had pushed out of the A Shau Valley were now literally starving, and they had nothing to lose. They must have figured, 'Let's just overrun this perimeter.' One of our ambush patrols got wiped out. They must have thought, 'We're going to die anyway, so let's take some Americans with us.'

"Later on, my buddies were busting my chops, because they had all gotten a week or so of R & R at some point and they went off to some tropic locale and drank like kings. But the army considered my visit to my father to be my R & R. When I finally did get back to the States, I was in Ft. Hood, Texas, on Thanksgiving weekend, and I got my paycheck and it was like, $2.50. I asked, 'Where did all my money go?' They said I had to reimburse them for that flight to California. By happenstance, it was my twenty-first birthday, so I bought myself a Schlitz tall boy and a couple of Slim Jims. That was my birthday dinner. But I was glad to be back in the USA."

Duggan's combat experience prepared him well for the job he took next: He joined the NYPD, working in the 44th precinct in the South Bronx, itself a war zone. One fellow cop was John Timoney, the future chief of department. Duggan soon made lieutenant, and with his then-wife had children, Jennifer and Ricky, who also became a police lieutenant. Later, he met beautiful Noreen O'Shea, who, like Tommy Collins's wife, Suzanne, was a pioneering female cop. They are together to this day, enjoying, finally, some well-deserved R & R.

When Chick found Bobby Pappas, he had what by any estimation was a big job. Pappas had gotten army training in radio and teletype communications so when he was deployed to Vietnam's 576th Ordinance Company in the Third Ordinance Battalion at Long Binh, he was made a sergeant and put in charge of all communications inside the ammunition depot—the world's largest. Working with the 25th Infantry's 89th MP Battalion, which guarded the depot, Pappas says, "We had thirty-two towers connected to us via radio and telephone" in an underground bunker. "We had six roving jeeps mounted with M2 50-caliber machine guns constantly patrolling the perimeter. We were in constant contact with them. We also had four dog handlers. The dogs would tell us if anybody was out there."

Even after the massive explosion Chick saw from twenty-five miles away at the start of the Tet offensive, when the Vietcong fired 122 millimeter rockets into the depot, killing four of Pappas's beloved officers in one hootch, the huge pyramids of ammunition remained primary targets.

"I would have to call in helicopter gunship support when it was needed," recalls Pappas. "On two occasions I had to call in napalm strikes."

Pappas remembers the day he left Vietnam: October 30, 1968. Like Collins, he notes, "They didn't give soldiers any debriefing. Boom, you're home, you're out. I think it doomed my marriage—I didn't see my wife and my baby daughter for the first year and a half."

Pappas went to work for the Long Island Lighting Co., becoming a project manager. After twenty-three years, he took a buyout, but they offered him a sweet deal to work as a private contractor. While his work life was good, his personal life was not. "I had nightmares every night. I couldn't sleep," Pappas says. "I was drinking heavily."

But then he made changes in his life that were akin to making a K-Turn midair with a C-130. "I stopped drinking in 1979 when I went into A.A. I started to get counseling for PTSD at the Veterans Administration. I still go. And I met and married Eileen."

That would be Eileen Tarpey, a nurse. "It's been great ever since I met her," Pappas attests. They share grandparenting duties from their home in Myrtle Beach, South Carolina, where Pappas golfs and goes fishing whenever he can. "I just hired a boat with four guys from A.A. and we went fishing on a lake. We caught nineteen catfish. It was a good day."

You could say that. Chick's buddies who survived left Vietnam, but for a long time, Vietnam didn't leave them. It took years, but they all seem to have built lives of joy. They deserve one good day after another.

The gang back together fifty years later at their old school in Inwood. From left to right: Rick Duggan, Tommy Collins, Chick Donohue, Kevin McLoone, and Bobby Pappas.

THE NEIGHBORHOOD–
INWOOD, MANHATTAN,
NEW YORK CITY

To understand how Chick Donohue could venture on his extraordinary journey to track down his buddies in combat, it helps to know the time and place from which they came. Urban planners would do well to study and replicate its attributes.

Chick and his buddies had the good fortune to grow up in Inwood, the unspoiled northern tip of Manhattan island, in the 1950s and early 1960s. Children played wild, free, and unattended, in virgin forest, in two rivers, and in all the streets between, yet it was New York City. With Big Nature only steps from the elevated subway, it was a magical place in a more innocent time, at once rural and urban, an oasis that Inwood native John F. McMullen, host of the online *JohnMac Radio Show*, has called "our end of heaven."

"We grew up at the entrance to Inwood Hill Park, where there were Indian caves," says Rick Duggan, who was twenty when Chick found him in combat in the Central Highlands of Vietnam in 1968 and who went on to become a New York Police Department lieutenant. "My mother used to tell me stories about an Indian princess who lived there when my mother was little."

Indeed, a Native American, Princess Noemie, lived in a cottage next to the three-hundred-year-old tulip tree the Lenape Indians considered sacred. A plaque today identifies it as the spot where Peter Minuit made his $24 deal of trinkets to buy Manhattan. (Generations of schoolchildren thought Minuit ripped off the Indians, but recent historians have postulated that it was Minuit who was scammed: he consummated the deal with Canarsee Indians chief Seysey, but it was the Lenape cousins, the Weckquaesgeeks Indians, who controlled that land.)

According to Cole Thompson's fascinating, picture-filled website My Inwood (myinwood.net), Princess Noemie taught Indian beadwork to the neighborhood children and hosted tribal gatherings as large as six hundred every September. In a neighboring cottage, Aimee LePrince Voorhees, daughter of Louis LePrince, the man who filmed the first moving image, also lived in the park. There she worked in her Indian-artifact-inspired Inwood Pottery Studio. Developer Robert Moses chopped down the sacred tulip tree and evicted Noemie and Aimee, but the spirit of place to which they contributed remained strong.

Inwood Hill Park had something you could find nowhere else in New York City, and still does: 196 acres of pristine old-growth forest, shading the ancient Native Americans' caves and the salt marsh they'd once fished. At the southern tip of the park stretches another sixty-six acres of nature called Fort

Tryon Park, home of the Cloisters Museum and its unicorn tapestries. John D. Rockefeller Jr. created the park out of old estates, gave it to the city, and, for good measure, bought the Palisades across the Hudson in New Jersey so that kids playing in the woods of Fort Tryon would see nothing but forest on the other side of the river as well.

To the north is Spuyten Duyvil (Dutch for "Swirling Devil") Creek; to the east, the Harlem River; and to the west, the mighty Hudson, all deemed swimmable by the children then. It was like living in an enchanted forest in the middle of the nation's biggest metropolis—an urban paradise worthy of Robin Hood and his Merry Men. Like that band of lads, Inwood kids stuck together.

"There were also baseball fields, even an Irish soccer field," recalled Tommy Collins, who was a military policeman when Chick found him in Qui Nhon and who became an NYPD cold-case detective after he came home. "We would play sports in there, run around, explore. It was a great place to grow up."

For those who found it hard to believe the Inwood scene in the 1995 movie version of *The Basketball Diaries*—in which Leonardo DiCaprio and Mark Wahlberg jump off a cliff into the Harlem River—doubt no longer. Collins recalls:

"We used to get the old inner tubes out of the gas stations, and if the attendant was nice, he would fix one for you. There was one fellow on 218th Street off Seaman Avenue who'd patch them for us. And we used to jump into the river and float across where the day liners used to come in."

A predominantly Irish and Jewish neighborhood, it produced such talents as basketball star Kareem Abdul-Jabbar, then known as Lew Alcindor; *The Basketball Diaries* author and punk rocker Jim Carroll; and Henry Stern, the commissioner and champion of New York City parks.

Like other parts of New York City at that time, Inwood was a neighborhood where large families lived side by side in small apartments, sharing celebrations and children's milestones, and looking out for one another whether their luck went up or down.

Eponymous restaurateur and Citi Field tavern owner Steve (Pally) McFadden, whose brother Joey was on Chick's list, said: "What I think made Inwood unique is that socially, everybody's family made the same amount of money. There was no 'rich' section, no 'poor' section.

"There was no outside pressure to wear or have expensive things you couldn't afford, like today," adds McFadden. "There was no pecking order. It put fewer pressures on people, so they could converse together. You could develop friendships with anybody."

"All the mothers hung their laundry on the roofs, next to one other," says Joe Reynolds, who served in Vietnam, and whose family owns historic Pete's Tavern in Gramercy Park.

Younger children, with mothers and neighbors watching from the windows or stoops, played skelly or ringolevio freely and safely for hours. When they got older, it was stickball or handball or team sports.

"There was no such thing as babysitting," says McFadden. "Older kids watched the younger kids; mothers put the littlest ones next door for an hour if they had to."

"Mostly, we all walked everywhere in the neighborhood," says Reynolds. "Mrs. Sullivan and her mother, who lived above the Blue Bakery, would put pillows on their windowsill and watch all the comings and goings. We'd yell up, 'Hey, Mrs. Sullivan, did you see Bobby Burns?' And she would say, 'Oh yes, Bobby went up that way about a half hour ago.'"

Families with six, eight, ten kids were not uncommon. You played with kids your age; your younger siblings and cousins played with their younger siblings in matching stair steps. You looked out for your friends' kid brothers and sisters as you would your own. You didn't have money, but you had one another.

As Seamus Heaney wrote, "If you have a strong first world and a strong set of relationships, then in some part of you, you are always free; you can walk the world because you know where you belong, you have some place to come back to."

BBQ AND A BEER-CAN SHOOT WITH A POWERFUL STRANGER

Kevin McLoone, the good Samaritan Chick found in Vietnam, had served four years in the US marines, and was one of the first in Vietnam, starting in 1963. McLoone returned to Vietnam to work for Dynalectron, the contractor tasked with installing the scrambling systems into the military helicopter radios to decrease the possibility of them being shot down. With that technological advancement, the war became very different.

In 1969, one year after Chick had encountered Kevin in the jungle and after they both survived the Tet offensive, the number of US soldiers in Vietnam peaked at more than a half million. Perhaps recognizing that McLoone and his coworkers had experienced some close calls as they hustled to make choppers safer in the midst of the fighting, the boss sent him on a choice assignment to one of Vietnam's most beautiful spots. It led to a bizarre encounter.

"A coworker named Bill and I were sent on a job to Vung Tau, an incountry place where guys went for R & R," McLoone recalls. "It was on the coast on a beautiful peninsula where a lot of the black-market people had mansions on the water. The French used to love Vung Tau—they called it Cap Saint-Jacques—and after we pulled out in 1975, oil was discovered offshore, and the Russians moved in."

After work one night, McLoone and Bill repaired to a bar. Inside, McLoone recounts, "We met a guy from the army who ran a Mike boat—an LCM-8, which, like the Higgins boats from World War II, were landing crafts that could open fully in the front to let tanks and trucks drive right onto the beach. He said they were having a lot of trouble with their radio communications with the Loran (long-range navigation) station on Con Son Island, about two hundred miles off the coast of southern Vietnam.[*] Secretary of Defense Robert McNamara had ordered that five of these radio towers (each roughly six hundred feet tall) be constructed throughout Southeast Asia to aid in long-range navigation of ships and planes in the era before we had global-positioning satellites.

"The Mike boat crew was about to depart to bring equipment to the coast guard station on Con Son Island," McLoone

---

[*] The sea off Con Son Island was also the place from which US Defense Attaché Richard Armitage, aboard the USS *Kirk*, went against orders in 1975 and led all thirty-two ships of the Republic of Vietnam navy, loaded with thirty thousand refugees, a thousand miles away to the Philippines the day after South Vietnam fell. So many choppers filled with additional refugees landed on the *Kirk*'s deck that sailors, after evacuating the refugees, pushed the choppers into the sea to make room for more. Armitage, a former naval officer, had to negotiate with the US and Philippine governments to allow the refugees to disembark.

recounts. "The officer asked us if we could take a few days off to go with them and help with their radio problems. We said okay and got clearance from our supervisor to help the army. I thought, *I wouldn't want to be out in the middle of the ocean with a bum radio.*

The Mike boat crew brought them up the Mekong River to the headquarters of the Ninth Infantry. "We got there during the night and refueled, and they picked up some equipment," McLoone recalls. "We were going to leave the next morning, when, all of a sudden, the place lit up. The base was being attacked with rockets, and a fuel dump had been hit. We were in the enlisted men's club on the base when the boat's warrant officer ran up and said, 'We gotta take off, or they're gonna sink the boat.' So, we hustled down to the river, and off we headed to the island."

The two-hundred-mile voyage was a long, overnight trip. "Bill and I were working on the radio below deck," McLoone recalls, "when halfway between the mainland and Con Son Island, I suddenly heard a loud noise and then a voice yelling, 'Identify yourself!' It was a US Navy Swift boat. Two army staff sergeants and two warrant officers were on our boat, and I heard one of them yelling, 'Get the hell out of here, you swab-bie!' and he was cursing at them. The Swift boat was off a navy destroyer, and the Mike boat was an army boat, and I guess there was a little competitiveness between the services. I ran up on deck and said to him, 'No, no, no; they're gonna sink us!' And I yelled to the guys in the Swift boat, 'Hey! We're Americans! Don't be hasty!' After a few minutes, they let us go."

They arrived at Con Son Island the next morning, at high tide. McLoone and his coworker had fixed the Mike boat's radio, and "everything was shipshape," he recalls. They were with the crew on deck, waiting for low tide, when the warrant officer came up to McLoone and said conspiratorially, "You know, I've got a case of frozen steaks and a whole bunch of beer on the boat."

"Outstanding!" McLoone replied.

"Let's have a barbecue after we unload all the equipment," the officer ventured.

"Sounds like a plan," McLoone concurred.

"There's one problem," the warrant officer said.

"Oh, what's that?"

"I've got all the good stuff, but I don't have charcoal. We're gonna be out here for a couple of hours, and I can't leave the boat. But you can. You gotta go in and find us some charcoal. It may take some time, so I suggest you leave now."

The warrant officer told McLoone that a coast guard lieutenant in charge of the unloading operation was waiting for them on the beach. The lieutenant might know where to find some charcoal, he suggested.

"All right," McLoone said. "I'll swim in, meet the guy, and I'll have the charcoal for you by the time you come in." The warrant officer gave a slow, wide smile, and McLoone jumped over the side and swam toward shore.

"It wasn't that far, maybe two hundred to three hundred yards," he recalls. "I grew up in Long Beach, New York, so I was a pretty decent swimmer. I emerged from the waves and met the coast guard lieutenant.

"'Sir,' I said, 'after the unloading operation, we're going to have a little soiree—you guys are invited, of course. But we're going to have to find a bag of charcoal.'"

The lieutenant was only too happy to help. They hopped in his jeep, and, to McLoone's surprise, they soon pulled up to the gates of a huge POW camp. The French had built Con Son Island prison in the eighteen hundreds, right after they built one on Devil's Island in French Guiana for the same purpose: to have an almost inescapable spot on which to keep political prisoners. In the 1930s, French colonial authorities had shipped a young Le Duan and his wingman Le Duc Tho out to this sandy hell, later exposed for its shallow tiger cages used to hold human prisoners lying in the sun. Le Duan and Le Duc Tho had plenty of time to make plans out on Con Son Island. Le Duan later became North Vietnam's chief military strategist and mastermind of the Tet offensive, and Le Duc Tho duked it out with US National Security Adviser Henry Kissinger during protracted peace talks, only to turn down the Nobel Prize they were both granted for negotiating the Paris Peace Accords that brought the war to a close on January 27, 1973.

"The lieutenant and I stood outside the gate, and he nodded toward the prisoners inside," McLoone recalls. "'He said, 'They'll get you charcoal.'"

"The South Vietnamese guards let us into the camp, and I was immediately surrounded by about twenty prisoners, each wearing a colored piece of cloth indicating whether they were North Vietnamese army regulars, Vietcong guerrillas, or non-military political prisoners. They looked at my feet and started pointing and laughing and saying, 'Ho! Ho!'"

"I had on what were called 'Ho Chi Minh sandals': flip-flops cut from rubber tires and laced with inner-tube straps. They were good for the boat because they supplied good traction. North Vietnamese soldiers wore them in the jungle; not even punji sticks could go through them. The POWs thought it was hysterical that I had them on. Then one of them asked in English, 'What do you want?'

"'I want charcoal,' I said."

The South Vietnamese prison guards would let the POWs chop down trees, cut them up, and burn them just enough to make charcoal and sell it to the US Coast Guard or the few other residents of the island. The prisoners used the money to pay for desperately needed food or other necessities, so the guards benefited.

"They sold me the charcoal for about two hundred *piastres*," McLoone recounts, "and I brought it back to the beach." By now, the Mike boat had landed, and the crew was unloading it. The warrant officer grinned at the sight of the charcoal, took it with thanks, and happily began firing up the grill.

"Bill and I were having a couple of cold ones on the beach," McLoone remembers, "when we saw three old DC-3 prop planes with South Vietnamese flags painted on the sides. They flew into the airstrip which the Japanese had built during World War II when they controlled Con Son Island. Then three South Vietnamese Swift boats pulled in, and they were just idling there. Suddenly a guy wearing mirrored aviator glasses and a baseball cap came strolling up the beach with a whole entourage, heading toward the Swift boats.

"Bill and I walked over to him, and I said, 'Hello, sir. What brings you here?'

"The wingmen looked at each other. The man with the mirrored shades said, 'I'm President Thieu.' He was as cool as a cucumber in a Frigidaire.

"'Well . . . How do you do?' I replied, trying to be formal. After all, I thought, this is General Nguyen van Thieu, the guy who runs the show. But Bill, he's from Greenville, South Carolina, he's a good ol' boy, and a great guy. He reached out and shook hands with Thieu and said, 'Pleased to meet ya!'

"We stood there for a minute. Finally, I said, 'Excuse me for asking, but what are you doing *here*?' I mean, it was pretty remote.

"Thieu answered, 'This is where I go fishing.'

"Whenever he could get away, he would try to relax by fishing off the island, he told us.

"'I'll tell you what,' Thieu added. 'If we catch some fish when we go out tonight, I'll give you some.'"

By now, the army crew had finished unloading, and it was playtime.

"We went back over to the crew, who were standing around the barbecue grill sipping beers as the warrant officer was tending the steaks.

"'What were you talking to *those* guys for?' the warrant officer asked us.

"Bill said, 'That's the president of South Vietnam right there!'

"'Yeah, right. Bull—!' the officer responded.

"'No, it really is Thieu,' I insisted. 'I recognize him from the newspapers.'

"'Damn it!' he swore. 'This tears it!'

"'Why?!' Bill asked.

"'Because now he's gonna wanna see the boat!'"

Who wouldn't? The seventy-ton boxy steel bruiser, built by Marinette Marine on the Menominee River in Wisconsin, could carry two Stryker armored fighting vehicles, or an M1 Abrams tank, or a herd of trucks or jeeps—any of which you could drive right into the surf off its drop-down bow.

The warrant officer ordered his men to put down their beers and return to the LCM-8 and start swabbing it down and putting everything in order. "They did it," McLoone recounts, "but they were not happy. Meanwhile, Thieu and his cadre took off on a motorboat, accompanied by the Swift boats. The crew got their boat spic-and-span and finally got to eat their steaks and have a few beers. By then, everybody was exhausted, so they went to sleep on the deck."

The next morning was a day off for the crew members, who were joking and laughing and seemed relieved that they wouldn't be doing anything official that day, much less giving a tour of the boat to Thieu and his officials. They took a swim and hung out on the sand for a while before the warrant officer fired up the grill again.

"Then, what do you know," McLoone recalls. "Along came President Thieu again, back down to the beach. He had a bunch of fish in his hand—I guess they do pretty well fishing at night out there. He handed us two huge red snappers, and we boned and filleted them and put them on the grill. We asked him if he would like a beer, and he took it, but then he handed it to one of his associates, who chugged it down. In Asia, I found, people don't want to offend anybody, for example, by rejecting a gift, so he accepted it, but delegated the actual drinking to an aide.

"Before long, the snappers and steaks were ready, and President Thieu and his men ate with us. Afterward, sure enough, he expressed curiosity about the Mike boat. We all boarded, and he took a look around and was impressed. We were hanging out on deck when one of Thieu's aides handed him a Remington Nylon .22 survival rifle and the aides started throwing empty beer cans—we had plenty of them—up in the air. Thieu started shooting at them.

"'I also like target practice,' Thieu said.

"Bill came up and said, 'Mind if I give it a try, Mr. President?'

"Bill might have been a hunter in South Carolina, because he was a great shot, and he would *ping!* the can every time. Thieu and Bill were handing the rifle back and forth, and the aides kept throwing cans up off the back of the boat, and they kept shooting them. I thought, *If the* New York Times *got a picture of this, with the POW camp up the road and the war going on, wow!* Bill had had a few beers by then, and I quietly said to him, 'Make sure you keep that thing pointed up.' Thieu's bodyguards were pretty on point all around him."

Then it was time to go, and the members of the two groups said their good-byes and went their separate ways. During the entire encounter, the president of South Vietnam hadn't said a word about the war going on in his country to the Americans who were there fighting in it.

"He didn't have to," concludes McLoone. "The war was obvious."

ACKNOWLEDGMENTS

We give thanks to Theresa O'Neill Donohue and George Rush and Eamon Rush for their patience and support. This book is written in memory of those we lost in Vietnam, including Chick's friends Michael F. Boyle, James Dziencilowski, Daniel J. Forster, John F. Knopf, Michael J. McGoldrick, John McHale, Thomas F. Minogue, Michael J. Morrow, Anthony J. O'Neill, Stephen V. Parker, Richard P. Reynolds Jr., Bernard Lynch, and J. T. Molloy's cousin, Eugene O'Connell.

Deepest thanks to Vietnam veterans Thomas (Tommy) Collins, Richard (Rick) Duggan, Robert (Bobby) Pappas, and Kevin McLoone for their service, and for sharing their vivid stories of meeting up with Chick in Vietnam.

Thank you to their partners in life, Suzanne Oquendo Collins, Noreen O'Shea, Eileen Pappas, and Margo McLoone, for all their participation and their own tales told.

Thanks to all those who helped Chick during his journey. Kudos to the late George "the Colonel" Lynch for conceiving it.

Our humble thanks to Mauro DiPreta, executive editor at William Morrow at HarperCollins Publishers, a modern-day Maxwell Perkins who made our book exponentially better with the help of his team: Vedika Khanna, Andrea Molitor, Phil Bashe, Pamela Barricklow, Liate Stehlik, Benjamin Steinberg, and Molly Waxman.

We are also grateful for the storytelling powers and editorial insights of Karen Duffy (Duff) Lambros, Malachy McCourt, Thomas Kelly, Robert Donohue, Jack Minogue, Coogan's owner and singer of Irish songs Peter Walsh, Joe Reynolds, Bill Wall of New York's Saluggi's and Nancy Whiskey Pub, Mila Andre, Seth Kaufman, Phil Cornell, John McMullen, and Audra Donohue O'Donovan; all the members of the Narrowbacks PFC Thomas Minogue Chapter, and the late Steve (Pally) McFadden.

Many thanks to New York's best literary agent, Frank Weimann at Folio Literary Management.

We feel great gratitude to talented filmmaker Andrew J. Muscato at Makuhari Productions for directing the documentary short of Chick's reunion with some of his beer-run buddies at the Piper's Kilt on West 231st Street in the Bronx. Also titled *The Greatest Beer Run Ever*, Muscato's film has garnered more than 625,000 views on YouTube as of 2020. Thanks to the Pabst Brewing Company for sponsoring the film.

Many thanks to Aimee Rivera, Don Granger, Dana Goldberg, and David Ellison of Skydance Media for believing that Chick's story should also be told in movie form; and to Oscar winners Peter Farrelly and Brian Hayes Currie, and Project Greenlight winner Pete Jones, for using their magic powers to conjure that.

Thanks to documentarian Eddie Rosenstein, Brian Donohue of the Laborers' International Union of North America

(LIUNA); and Sean Donohue of the International Union of Operating Engineers (IUOE).

Thanks to the savvy strategists at DKCNews public relations, including Sean Cassidy, Joe DePlasco, Carolyn Petschler, Michael Moschella, and Nathan Adams for bringing this story to more people; and to financial wizards Norman Dawidowicz and Lesley Grannum for helping to make that a reality.

Thanks to attorney Michael Carroll of O'Dwyer and Bernstein; publishing lawyers Sheila and Gerald Levine; and entertainment lawyers Jonathan Horn; and Robert M. Szymanski of Eclipse Law Corp. for their expert legal advice.

Many thanks to Philadelphia's Irish Pub owner Mark O'Connor and his trusty aide Allie Pfender. In Philadelphia, O'Connor had the brilliant idea to hold "The Shortest Beer Run Ever" between his Irish Pub at 2007 Walnut Street and his Irish Pub at 1123 Walnut Street to raise money for the Marine Corps–Law Enforcement Foundation, which benefits children. Those of us from *The Greatest Beer Run* team were humbled to participate with Medal of Honor recipients Mike Thornton, Barney Barnum, and Brian Thacker as they raced the course in Humvees, led by the Philadelphia Police Department. Small wonder that O'Connor's Irish Pub Children's Foundation has raised $5 million for charity.

Only 0.5 percent of Americans serve in the military, but 100 percent of us benefit. Thank you.

BIBLIOGRAPHY

Associated Press. "2D Blast in Saigon Wounds Eight GIs Near Bombed Ship." *New York Times*, May 3, 1964.

Bao, Ninh. *The Sorrow of War: A Novel of North Vietnam*. Edited by Frank Palmos. Translated from the Vietnamese by Phan Thanh Hao. New York: Riverhead Books, 1996.

Buckley, Tom. "Foe Invades U.S. Embassy, Raiders Wiped Out After 6 Hours, Vietcong Widen Attack on Cities, Ambassador Safe, Guerrillas Also Strike Presidential Palace and Many Bases." *New York Times*, January 31, 1968.

Butler, Gen. Smedley D. Butler. *War Is a Racket*. Chicago: Aristeus Books, 2014. First published 1935 by Round Table Press (New York).

Daverde, Alex. "The Real Pentagon Papers." National Archive National Declassification Center online. *The NDC Blog*. Last modified May 26, 2011. declassification.blogs.archives.gov/2011/05/26/the-real-pentagon-papers.

Do, Kiem, and Julie Kane. *Counterpart: A South Vietnamese Naval Officer's War*. Annapolis, MD: Naval Institute Press, 1998.

Du, Nguyen. *The Tale of Kieu: A New Cry from a Broken Heart* (epic poem). Translated by Le-Xuan-Thuy. Glendale, CA: Dai Nam, 1988.

FitzGerald, Frances. *Fire in the Lake: The Vietnamese and the Americans in Vietnam*. Repr. ed. Boston: Back Bay Books, 2002. First published 1972 by Atlantic–Little Brown (Boston).

Halberstam, David. *The Best and the Brightest*. New York: Ballantine Books, 1972.

Herr, Michael. *Dispatches*. Repr. ed. New York: Vintage Books, 1991. First published 1977 by Knopf (New York).

Horodysky, T. "American Merchant Marine at War." Last modified June 24, 2019. Usmm.org. An invaluable online resource on the Merchant Marine, authored by heroic Merchant Mariner advocate Ms. Tamara (Toni) Horodysky.

Karnow, Stanley. *Vietnam: A History*. New York: Penguin Books, 1983.

Luce, Don. "The Tiger Cages of Vietnam." Historians Against the War online. https://www.historiansagainstwar.org/resources/torture/luce.html.

Mohr, Charles. "U.S. Aide in Embassy Villa Kills Guerrilla with Pistol." *New York Times,* January 31, 1968.

Napoli, Philip F. *Bringing It All Back Home: An Oral History of New York City's Vietnam Veterans*. New York: Hill and Wang, 2014.

Nguyen, Lien-Hang. "Exploding the Myths About Vietnam." *New York Times,* August 11, 2012.

North, Don. "Don North: An American Reporter Witnessed the VC Assault on the U.S. Embassy During the Vietnam War." *Vietnam*, February 2001.

Oberdorfer, Don. *Tet!: The Turning Point in the Vietnam War*. Rev. ed. Baltimore: Johns Hopkins University Press, 2001.

Olson, Wyatt. "Saigon Embassy Attack: 'They're Coming In!' " Washington, D.C., Stars and Stripes, Stripes.com, January 17, 2018. https://www.stripes.com/news/special-reports/1968-stories/remembering-the-saigon-embassy-attack-50-years-later-they-re-coming-in-1.507103.

Rhodes, James. "Vietnam's Con Dao [Con Son Island] Prison, Then and Now." *L.A. Progressive*. Last modified January 2, 2015. https://www.laprogressive.com/page/2/?s=James+Rhodes.

Roush, Gary. "Statistics About the Vietnam War." Vietnam Helicopter Flight Crew Network online. Last modified June 2, 2008. http://vhfcn.org/stat.html.

Rovedo, Michael. "Tet Offensive of 1968." Military Police of the Vietnam War online. http://www.militarypolicevietnam.com. Accessed December 2019.

Safer, Morley. *Flashbacks: On Returning to Vietnam*. New York: Random House, 1990.

Sheehan, Neil. *A Bright Shining Lie*. New York: Vintage Books, 1989.

Sigalos, MacKenzie. "The Vietnam War: How They Saw It from Both Sides of the Divide." CNN online. Last modified May 23, 2016. https://www.cnn.com/2016/05/23/asia/america-vietnam-view-vietnam-war/index.html.

Steinman, Ron. *The Soldiers' Story: An Illustrated Edition; Vietnam in Their Own Words*. New York: Book Sales Inc., 2015.

Sterling, Eleanor Jane, Martha Maud Hurley, and Le Duc Minh. *Vietnam: A Natural History*. Illustrated by Joyce A. Powzyk. New Haven, CT: Yale University Press, 2007.

Stone, Jim. "Beer & Soda Available During the Vietnam War: A Welcome Break from the Hardships." Mobile Riverine Force Association online. Last modified March 15, 2003. https://www.mrfa.org/us-navy-army/beer-soda-available-during-the-vietnam-war.

Swancer, Brent. "The Mysterious Rock Apes of the Vietnam War." Mysterious Universe online. Last modified January 29, 2016. https://mysteriousuniverse.org/2016/01/the-mysterious-rock-apes-of-the-vietnam-war.

Tang, Truong Nhu, David Chanoff, and Doan Van Toai. *A Viet Cong Memoir: An Inside Account of the Vietnam War and Its Aftermath*. New York: Vintage Books, 1986.

Telfer, Maj. Gary L., Lt. Col. Lane Rogers, and Dr. V. Keith Fleming Jr. *U. S. Marines in Vietnam: Fighting the North Vietnamese—1967*. Washington, DC: History and Museums Division, Headquarters, U.S. Marines Corps, 1984. https://www.marines.mil/Portals/1/Publications/U.S.%20Marines%20in%20Vietnam%20Fighting%20the%20North%20Vietnamese%201967%20%20PCN%2019000309000_1.pdf.

Thompson, Cole. "Inwood: The Bar Scene of Not So Long Ago." My Inwood. Last modified March 24, 2014. http://myinwood.net/inwood-the-bar-scene-of-not-so-long-ago. Website maintained by passionate Inwood historian, broker Cole Thompson.

Tucker, Spencer C., ed. *The Encyclopedia of the Vietnam War: A Political, Social, & Military History*. New York: Oxford University Press, 1998.

Tuchman, Barbara W. *The March of Folly: From Troy to Vietnam*. New York: Alfred A. Knopf, 1984.

US Army online. "Medal of Honor: Command Sergeant Major Bennie Adkins." https://www.army.mil/medalofhonor/adkins.

US National Archives and Records Administration online. "Vietnam War U.S. Military Fatal Casualty Statistics." Last modified April 30, 2019. archives.gov/research/military/vietnam-war/casualty-statistics.

Valentine, Tom. "Vietnam War Draft." July 25, 2013: TheVietnamWar. info/vietnam-war-draft.

Wendt, E. Allan, foreign services officer and eyewitness. "Viet Cong Invade American Embassy—The 1968 Tet Offensive." Association for Diplomatic Studies and Training online. Accessed February 2017. https://adst.org/2013/07/viet-cong-invade-american-embassy-the-1968-tet-offensive. First published November 3, 1981, by the *Wall Street Journal*.

Westmoreland, William C. *A Soldier Reports*. New York: Doubleday, 1976.

VIDEO

Abbott, John, dir. *Action in Vietnam* (documentary). Available on YouTube. Made by Australian Commonwealth Film Unit, 1966. 25:01. Uploaded by MFSA Films. https://www.youtube.com/watch?v=6E2-OOQo13c.

Burns, Ken, and Lynn Novick, dirs. *The Vietnam War* (documentary). 10-part series. Aired September 17, 2017–September 28, 2017, on PBS.

Davis, Peter, dir. *Hearts and Minds* (documentary). 1974. Rainbow Pictures.

Ellison, Richard, prod., *Vietnam: A Television History*. 13-part series produced by WGBH public television in Boston. First aired 1983.

PHOTO CREDITS

All photographs by the author unless stated below.